GNVQ FOUNDATION Business

Sharon Murphy
Jacqueline Palmer

with contributions by
Alec Main and Christine Woodrow

Edited by
Alison Atkinson
Keith Brumfitt
Duncan Cullimore

Thomas Nelson and Sons Ltd
Nelson House Mayfield Road
Walton-on-Thames Surrey
KT12 5PL UK

Nelson Blackie
Wester Cleddens Road
Bishopbriggs
Glasgow
G64 2NZ UK

Thomas Nelson Australia
102 Dodds Street
South Melbourne
Victoria 3205 Australia

Nelson Canada
1120 Birchmount Road
Scarborough Ontario
M1K 5G4 Canada

© Sharon Murphy and Jacqueline Palmer 1995

First published by Thomas Nelson and Sons Ltd 1995

I(T)P Thomas Nelson is an International Thomson Publishing Company.

I(T)P is used under licence.

ISBN 0–17–490003–1

NPN 9 8 7 6 5 4 3 2 1

All rights reserved. No paragraph of this publication may be reproduced, copied or transmitted save with written permission or in accordance with the provisions of the Copyright, Design and Patents Act 1988, or under the terms of any licence permitting limited copying issued by the Copyright Licensing Agency, 90 Tottenham Court Road, London, W1P 9HE.

The publisher grants permission for copies of pages 32, 33, 34, 97 and 98 to be made without fee as follows:

Private purchasers may make copies for their own use or for use by their own students; school purchasers may make copies for use within and by the staff and students of the institution only.
This permission to copy does not extend to additional institutions or branches of an institution, who should purchase a separate master copy of the book for their own use.
For copying in any other circumstances prior permission must be obtained in writing from Thomas Nelson and Sons Ltd.

Printed in Spain.

Acknowledgements
Illustrations and other printed matter
The authors and publishers are grateful to the following for permission to reproduce copyright material. If any acknowledgement has been omitted, this will be rectified at the earliest possible opportunity.

Page 54: receipt reproduced by permission of TGI Fridays – the American restuarant and bar; counterfoils reproduced by permission of National Westminster Bank.
Page 72, logos reproduced by permission of: Abbey National; Apex Car Hire (Nick Clark); The Beauty Shop; C&A; Interflora (the Interflora roundel is owned by FTD Incorporated and Interflora [FTDA] British Unit Ltd, Sleaford, Lincolnshire is a registered user in the United Kingdom); Mitsubishi Motors; Oxfam; RAC; Surrey Building Supplies.

The authors and publishers are grateful to the following organisations for their co-operation in the production of this book:
Page 43: Safeway plc.
Page 106: Filofax Group plc. Filofax is the registered trademark of Filofax Group plc.
Page 107: The British School of Motoring (BSM).

Photographs
ARP: p. 4 (top and centre)
David Bamber: pp. 40, 43, 53, 62, 90, 91, 95, 109, 110
J Allan Cash: p. 7
Andrew Ross: pp. 4 (bottom two), 5, 8, 9, 10, 14, 63, 106
Cover photograph: GNVQ Business students at John Ruskin College, photographed by Len Cross.

The Foundation GNVQ Business Team
Authors
Sharon Murphy, Totton College.
Jacqueline Palmer, John Ruskin College.
Editors
Alison Atkinson, Keith Brumfitt and Duncan Cullimore, School of Education, University of Brighton.
Contributors
Alec Main, Thomas Danby College.
Christine Woodrow, Huddersfield New College.

Advisers
Amyn Abdulla, Personnel Department, Marks and Spencer plc, Croydon.
Jo Clark, Personnel Department, Marks and Spencer plc, Croydon.
Mike Hemmings, Seaford Head Community College.
Elizabeth Louden-Brown, Mid Kent College of H & FE.
Kevin Maskell, John Ruskin College.
Liz Norris, Mid Kent College of H & FE.

Contents

How to use this book — v
Finding the information you need — v

Introduction — vi
What is GNVQ? — vi
What is Foundation GNVQ Business? — vi
How do you learn on your GNVQ? — vi
How is your GNVQ assessed? — vi

Toolkit — 1

General information — 2
Study skills — 2
Solving problems — 2
Carrying out research — 4
Writing questionnaires — 5
Improving your grading – some helpful hints — 6
Health and safety — 7

Communication — 8
Listening skills — 8
Talking skills — 9
Talking on the telephone — 9
Making presentations — 9
Body language — 11
Writing skills — 12
Formal letters — 12
Memoranda (memos) — 13
Using images — 14
Simple reports — 14

Application of Number and Information Technology — 15
Percentages — 15
VAT — 16
Discounts — 16
Pictorial presentation — 18
Bar charts — 18
Pictograms — 20
Measure — 21
Systems of measurement — 21
Metric and imperial — 21
Paper — 23
Conversion — 24
Conversion factors — 24
Conversion tables and graphs — 24
Using information technology — 26
Using a spreadsheet — 26
Safety first! — 28
The mean, the mode and the range — 29
The mean — 29
The mode — 29
The range — 30
Answers — 31

Forms for you to fill in — 32
Application form — 32
Invoice — 33
Cheque — 33
Credit card sales voucher — 34
Paying-in slip — 34
Cash book — 34

Unit 1: Processing business payments — 35

Explore ways of processing payments — 36
Why are payments made in business? — 36
Ways of making and processing payments — 37
Cash — 37
Cheques — 38
Debit cards — 40
Credit cards — 41
Electronic transfer of funds — 42
Case study: Safeway supermarket — 43
Paying-in slips — 44
Keeping payment records — 45
The purpose of payment documents — 45
Why is it important to keep accurate payment records? — 47
Assignment: Wright's Corner Shop — 48

Produce and check payment documents — 49
Producing invoices — 49
What's on an invoice? — 49
Discounts — 50
Value added tax — 50
Checking invoices — 51
Methods of paying invoices — 53
Cash — 53
Cheque — 53
Debit card — 53
Credit card — 53
Documents which prove payment has been made — 54
Checking documents — 54
Assignment: Cristal's Health Club — 55

Maintain payment records — 56
Keeping a record of payments — 56
How do businesses keep records? — 57
Manual or computerised? — 57
What records do businesses keep? — 57
Payments received sheets — 58
Checking a payments received sheet — 58
Cash books — 59
Paying money into the bank — 59
Withdrawing money from the bank — 60
Checking a cash book balances — 60
Cash discounts — 62
Case study: Cakes and buns — 62
Case study: The GNVQ tuck shop — 63

How can you tell if you are keeping accurate records?	64
Assignment: The Strange Sports Shop	64
Quiz: How much do you know about business payments?	65

Unit 2: Investigating business and customers 67

Describe businesses and customers 68

Why do businesses exist and what do they do?	68
Desert island living	69
Businesses for profit	70
Businesses not for profit	70
Businesses for charity	70
What's around the corner from you?	71
Goods and services	72
The customer is always right	74
Customer service	74
What customers expect of businesses	75
Assignment: Local business survey	77
Quiz: How much do you know about businesses and their customers?	78

Investigate costs and profit in business 79

Factors which affect profit	80
Case study: Yvonne's flower shop	80
Categories of business costs	81
Costs which stay the same	82
Costs which don't stay the same	82
Case study: Yvonne's business costs	82
How do employees contribute to business profit?	83
How to improve profitability	83
How can employees benefit from business profit?	85
What are the main types of benefit?	85
Assignment: Desktop	87
Quiz: How much do you know about costs and profits?	88

Make a sales presentation to a customer 89

What is a sales presentation?	89
Stages in the selling process	90
Knowing the product	91
Answering questions about the product	92
Ways of paying	93
After-sales service	93
Guarantees	94
Making a presentation to sell a product	94
Case study: The tale of the first-time presenter	95
An effective presentation	95
Make sure you prepare well	95
The presentation: the 10-point plan	96
Assessing your presentation	97
Assignment: Making your first sales presentation	98
Quiz: How good are you at sales presentations?	99

Unit 3: Investigating working in business 101

Business organisations and personnel in departments 102

Types of business organisations – who owns what?	102
Sole trader – be your own boss	103
Case study: Paula is a success, could you be?	103
Partnerships – two heads are better than one	104
Private limited companies – 'up and coming'	105
Public limited company – the premier division	106
Case study: Filofax – 'wonder of the 80s: success of the 90s'	106
Franchise – a small part of a bigger whole	107
Case study: British School of Motoring (BSM)	107
Co-operatives – working together	107
Local authority services	107
Business departments – where things get done	108
Job titles and their responsibilities – who does what?	109
What are people in charge of?	109
Assignment: Chamber of Commerce competition	111
Quiz: How much do you know about business organisations?	112

Investigate jobs in business 113

Help! I need some advice	113
What shall I do?	114
Suitable jobs – for now and later	116
Finding the right job	116
What are employers looking for?	117
Suitable jobs for suitable people	118
Skills for jobs	119
Qualifications for jobs	120
How to get those qualifications	121
Assignment: Newspaper article	122
Quiz: How much do you know about investigating jobs?	123

Plan for employment in business 124

Help!	124
Personal information – giving the right details	124
A job which asks for a CV	125
Ways to find out about jobs	127
You have found the job, now what happens?	128
The five-point plan of recruitment	128
How else might I have to apply for a job?	129
Letters of application	129
Application forms	130
Assignment: The careers exhibition	131
Quiz: What do you know about planning for jobs?	132

Useful addresses and organisations 133

Quiz answers 134

Core skills coverage grid 135

Index 136

How to use this book

This book contains information, ideas and activities for Foundation GNVQ Business students. It covers:
- the three mandatory units (Units 1, 2 and 3)
- the level 1 core skills in Application, Communication and Information Technology
- vocabulary and skills you will find useful throughout your GNVQ, and when you start work or go on to take another course.

Finding the information you need

You will see that this book is divided into four main sections:
- the Toolkit. This contains general information on how to approach GNVQ assignments and activities; advice to help you achieve the core skills units in Application of Number, Communication and Information Technology; and business forms which you can photocopy and practise filling in
- Unit 1: Processing business payments
- Unit 2: Investigating business and customers
- Unit 3: Investigating working in business.

Each of the Unit sections covers all the elements, performance criteria and range statements you need to understand for your GNVQ.

Recognising symbols

This book uses symbols to help you find different types of information and activities. Look out for the following.

What to look for — **What it means**

Activity. There is an activity on most pages to help you practise skills and find out more information.

Case study. Some sections include case studies to help you understand how things work in the real world of business.

Assignment. At the end of every element there is an assignment. If you complete this assignment, you will produce some useful evidence for your portfolio.

Quiz. Quizzes are included for fun, but they are a useful way to show how well you have understood the information in the mandatory units.

Question. Something for you to think about, or a question for you to answer.

What does it mean? An explanation of business words which might be new to you.

More information. Often, topics are covered in more than one place in this book. Where it would be useful for you to look at another page for more information, you will see this symbol.

Introduction

What is GNVQ?

GNVQ stands for General National Vocational Qualification. All GNVQ qualifications cover a broad area of the world of work, such as 'business', 'manufacturing' or 'leisure and tourism'. Each year, tens of thousands of students take GNVQ courses.

You can take GNVQs at three levels:
- Foundation
- Intermediate
- Advanced.

You are studying for a Foundation GNVQ. This can:
- help you decide which career to follow
- prepare you for your chosen career
- give you a nationally recognised qualification
- put you on the ladder to further qualifications.

When you have completed your Foundation GNVQ in Business, you will probably either find employment or go on to an Intermediate GNVQ (this could be in Business or another GNVQ subject).

What is Foundation GNVQ in Business?

Foundation GNVQ in Business is about what people in business do and the skills they need.

These skills include:
- understanding business ideas and terms
- being enterprising and working well as part of a team. Enterprise means drive and good ideas; teamwork means pulling together. If you are going to be involved in business management, you have to be enterprising and you have to be a good teamworker
- communicating well, working with numbers, and using information technology.

Your GNVQ – and this book – will introduce you to all of these skills, and will put you on the road to developing them for yourself.

How do you learn on your GNVQ?

You will already have realised that studying for a GNVQ is different to studying for a GCSE. This is partly because it is about work outside school or college, but it is also because the course is written in terms of performance criteria, range statements and evidence indicators.

Your teacher will have a full copy of what you need to achieve for your GNVQ, and during the course you will probably be given a copy as well. You will need this so you can plan how to show you have gained the skills, knowledge and understanding described in the evidence indicators.

You already know that you need to be organised in order to collect and store the evidence of your achievements in a portfolio. You also need to organise your own learning through 'action planning'. This does not mean your teacher is out of a job; but it does mean that you will have more say than ever before in how you learn.

Action planning takes place every time you tackle a new topic. Your teacher will suggest activities to you that are related to the evidence indicators, and you will be asked to plan an activity – either on your own, or as part of a group. You need to make sure that the activity covers the performance criteria, range statements and evidence indicators.

How is your GNVQ assessed?

Your GNVQ is assessed in two ways.
- You collect your coursework in a portfolio of evidence, which you have to organise carefully so it meets the evidence indicators. Your teacher will help you do this, but you are responsible for the portfolio so you must be well organised. This portfolio is then assessed to make sure that you have covered all the performance criteria and range statements for each unit, and that you have met the evidence indicators.
- You take three one-hour short answer tests covering the three mandatory units. If you don't pass these first time you can take them again, but you must pass them in order to achieve your GNVQ.

Toolkit

Introduction

This Toolkit contains information to help you work towards your Foundation Business GNVQ. As you read this book, you will probably find it useful to look back to this section for ideas, advice and information.

The Toolkit includes:
- general information on how to approach GNVQ assignments and activities
- advice and information to help you achieve the core skills units in Communication, Application of Number and Information Technology
- photocopiable resources you can use to practise different skills as you work through the book.

Toolkit

General information

This section looks at some of the skills and knowledge you will need for your GNVQ. It includes information on:
- study skills – how to approach your GNVQ course
- carrying out research – how to find the information you need for assignments and activities
- improving your grades – how to get the result you want at the end of the course.

It also includes a section on health and safety, which plays an important part in the day-to-day running of businesses.

Study skills

As soon as you start your Foundation GNVQ, you will probably find that you need to study in new ways. You may find this difficult at first.

Solving problems

What shall I do? How shall I do it?
- **Ask** – your teacher.
- **Ask** – your friends.
- **Ask** – other people.

I need some information, but I don't know where to find it.
- Read pages 4 and 5 of the Toolkit.
- Try asking people (see above).
- Look in the library or learning centre.

I don't understand the book I'm reading.
- See if someone else can explain it to you.
- See if you can find another book which is easier to read.
- Do you need to read the book? Perhaps you can find another way of getting the information. Try a CD-ROM or a newspaper.

I've found a book that helps, but I can't find the piece of information I'm looking for.
- Try the contents pages at the front of the book. The chapter headings may help you.
- Look at the index at the back of the book.

The computer won't do what I want.
- See if there's a manual or a worksheet you can use.
- Find 'Help' on the menu and see if that gives you some ideas.
- Is there anyone else in the room who knows what to do?

General information

I've got to interview someone and I'm nervous.
- Write out an interview plan in advance.
- Make sure you have a firm appointment.
- Take a friend with you, if possible.

I've got to give a presentation and I'm worried about it.
- Read pages 9 and 10 of the Toolkit.
- Be well prepared.
- Don't let your friends in the audience put you off or make you giggle.

I've got to phone a business.
- Say who you are and whom you want to talk to.
- Know exactly what you want to ask.
- Say thank you and goodbye at the end of the conversation.

I've got to write a business letter.
- Check that you know the correct way to lay out a business letter.
- Always word process it, and use the spell check before printing.
- Use headed paper, or make sure that your name and address are on the letter.

I don't enjoy writing reports and assignments.
- Ask if you can give a presentation instead.
- Talk to your tutor about how you feel and what you can do about it.
- Think about why you don't like writing. Do you need a better pen? Do you need some help with spelling? Try to write only a small amount at a time.

I'm not very good at spelling.
- If you word process your work, spell check **everything**.
- Ask a friend or tutor to read work and point out mistakes, or use a dictionary to check it for yourself.
- Ask your tutor if you can have extra help.

Toolkit

Carrying out research

You might wonder where to find the information you need to complete work for your GNVQ. Here are some suggestions.

- If you want to find out about types of companies which trade locally, try looking in the *Yellow Pages* or *Thomson Directory* for your area.
- **Books** are a good way to find information. You don't have to read a whole textbook to find what you're looking for. Try reading the **list of contents** to see if the chapter headings tell you where to look. If not, then most books have an **index** at the back of the book. Look up a word in the index (for instance, you could look up 'debit card') and you should find the page number on which you can find more information. 
- A good place to find information which is not in the book you are using is the **local library**. Librarians will be able to help you find different **books** and other sources of information on the subjects you're interested in. For instance, most libraries now have a **CD-ROM** available. You'll find that there are whole encyclopaedias available on CD-ROM, with pictures and photographs which you can print out for your portfolio. 
- Libraries have copies of the **electoral register** for your area. This is very useful if you need information like how many houses or flats there are with only one person living in them, or how many houses or flats there are in a certain street or area. Most libraries will also have copies of **laws** and **acts** which affect businesses. You may not be able to take these away, but you will be able to read them in the library.
- You could try asking questions at your **local town hall**. A lot of information is kept there; for example, how much business tax costs locally. The local **inspector of weights and measures** will be able to give you details of rules about cleanliness in shops, and what should happen if you have to return something you've bought. You will also find

4

General information

that your town hall has a **planning officer** who will be able to tell you about any planned buildings in your area, such as a new superstore or shopping centre. All of these people are very busy, and it is important that you make an appointment before you try to interview them.

- For financial matters, you will find your local **banks** very helpful. High street banks include Barclays, Lloyds, Midland and National Westminster. All have **leaflets** which will tell you how to set up and run businesses, and how to get loans for business purposes. Often **bank staff** will be willing to talk to you if you have particular questions.

Writing questionnaires

Questionnaires can be a good way to find out information, but watch out! It's easy to write questionnaires that don't find out the information you really want. For your questionnaires at Foundation level, try following these simple rules.

- Keep your questionnaire short.
- Make sure that you ask for **all** the information you need. Compare your questionnaire with an outline of what you want to find out.
- Lay out your questionnaire so it is easy to read.
- Decide whether you're going to put your questions face to face, or give people a questionnaire form to fill in.
- Test your questionnaire on a small group of people before you use it.
- Rewrite any questions they don't understand.

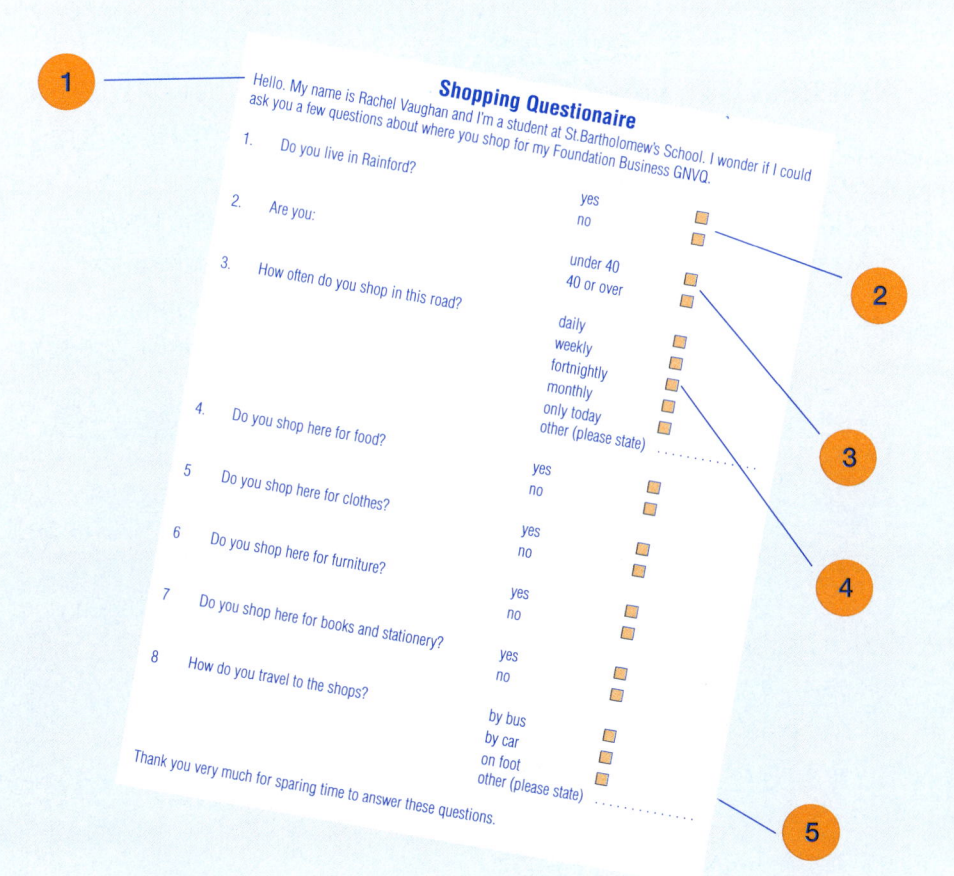

Shopping Questionnaire

Hello. My name is Rachel Vaughan and I'm a student at St.Bartholomew's School. I wonder if I could ask you a few questions about where you shop for my Foundation Business GNVQ.

1. Do you live in Rainford? yes / no
2. Are you: under 40 / 40 or over
3. How often do you shop in this road? daily / weekly / fortnightly / monthly / only today / other (please state)
4. Do you shop here for food? yes / no
5. Do you shop here for clothes? yes / no
6. Do you shop here for furniture? yes / no
7. Do you shop here for books and stationery? yes / no
8. How do you travel to the shops? by bus / by car / on foot / other (please state)

Thank you very much for sparing time to answer these questions.

1 Explain why you're carrying out a survey.
2 Ask closed questions; either questions which can be answered by 'yes' or 'no', or multiple choice questions.
3 Make sure that your questions won't upset anyone. Asking a person's age outright might seem rude.
4 If necessary, suggest alternatives.
5 Thank people for their help.

5

Toolkit

Improving your grading – some helpful hints

To get a merit or distinction grading for your GNVQ, you will need to think about four points:
- planning your work
- presenting and understanding information
- the quality of your work
- evaluating your work.

None of these is difficult, but you will need to bear them in mind as you work on assignments and activities.

Planning
1. Always plan carefully what you are going to do and discuss it with your tutor.
2. Decide in what order to carry out tasks.
3. Set yourself deadlines by which you must do things.
4. Spread your work out sensibly – don't try to do everything just before work is due in!
5. Always write down your plan.
6. Keep your plan at the front of your work so that you know where it is.

Information
1. Where possible, use computers to produce work.
2. Always keep a record of research you have done and information you have collected.
3. Keep all the information for one unit together.
4. If you have to do any maths, try to use a calculator or a spreadsheet.
5. Make sure that all information is presented as neatly as possible.
6. Always say where you found information.

Quality
1. Make sure that you have done everything you were asked to do.
2. Write clearly using good English and the correct business words.
3. Make sure that you have done the best you can, not the least you can get away with.
4. Get your work in on time.

Evaluation
1. Go to tutorials and review sessions, and listen to what your tutors say. Take notes.
2. When you have finished a piece of work, look at your plan and see if you followed it. If not, why not?
3. Think about whether you would do something differently next time. If so, what would it be and why?
4. Did you enjoy the work? If not, why not? Was it too difficult? Too easy? Could you have made it more interesting?
5. Did you find it useful? What did you learn? This **might not** be obvious at first. For instance, you might have learned that you have the confidence to do something you thought you couldn't do.

General information

Health and safety

Health and safety is an important part of everyone's working life. If your job involves you in any dangerous activity, then it is the law that your employer provides you with safety equipment. For instance, if you are using an industrial guillotine to cut large quantities of paper or material, you will be given chain-link gloves to wear to protect your fingers from the blade.

It is also the employer's responsibility to provide a healthy working environment, and if the workplace becomes too hot or too cold then workers cannot be required to work there.

Trade unions often bring health and safety issues to the attention of a company's management. However, there is a law which gives clear directions on what a business must do to make sure that its employees are safe and well.

This is called the **Health and Safety at Work Act 1974** (the date is different if you live in Northern Ireland).

- The Act covers all places of work, including factories, shops, farms, colleges and schools.
- If there is a recognised trade union, it should appoint someone to be the employees' safety representative, who will try to make sure that the Act is carried out.
- Employers must make the place of work as safe as possible, and supply safety equipment where necessary.
- There are particular rules about handling dangerous substances.
- It is the responsibility of both employers and employees to make sure that working practices are safe.

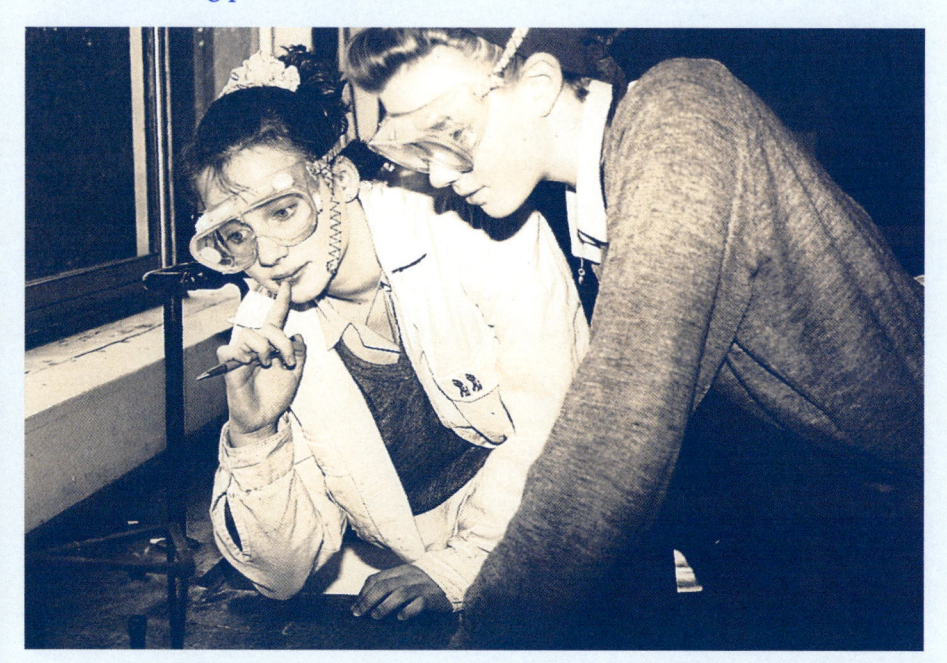

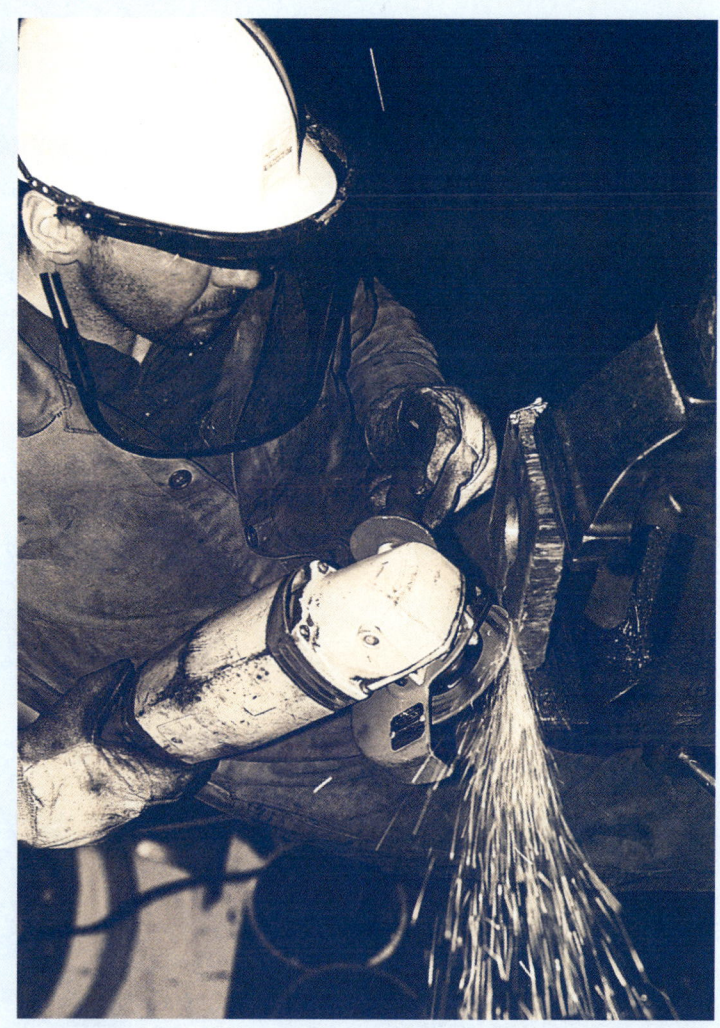

By law, employers must provide their workers with the safety equipment they need

The Health and Safety at Work Act applies in schools and colleges, as well as in the workplace

Toolkit

Communication

Good communication skills are very important in business. To work in business, you will need to be able to talk and write to a wide range of people in many different ways.

For instance, you will need to talk to people on the telephone, in meetings, during interviews and when giving presentations. You will also need to be a good listener, which is why this section starts with listening skills.

Listening skills

Be an active listener. Look at the person who is talking. Nod and smile when you agree. Face the person, and lean forward slightly in your chair to show that you are interested.

If you can, make sure that the setting for an **interview** or **discussion** is as good as possible:

- avoid distractions like rattling window blinds or a flickering light
- remove barriers like large desks or tables
- create comfort to try to put the other person at ease. Sit in armchairs and provide coffee.

Your **body language** should show that you are interested and alert:

- look at the person speaking – but don't stare
- give appropriate prompts – nods, facial expressions, 'uh-huh', 'go on'
- uncross your arms and legs
- make sure your voice sounds interested
- ask questions – it helps others to focus their thoughts.

Soon afterwards, make notes of the important points made during the discussion.

For more on body language, see page 11.

Communication

Talking skills

People who work in business need to talk to a wide range of people on different subjects.

Talking on the telephone

Remember: no one can see you smile or frown over the telephone, so make sure your voice and the words you use send clear messages.

Preparing for the call

1. Get a pen and paper so you can make notes.
2. Check that you have the phone number and extension.
3. Check the name and job title of the person you're calling.
4. Prepare a list of questions to ask.
5. Decide what information you want them to provide.
6. Make sure you know your number in case they need to return your call.
7. Check that you know your address – including the postcode – for any written reply.

The call itself

1. Give your name, and explain briefly why you are calling.
2. Give the name and job title of the person to whom you wish to speak.
3. Repeat (1) if necessary. When you ring a business, the call will often need to be transferred – make sure you don't off-load all your questions or information on the wrong person.
4. Ask your questions and/or give your information.
5. Speak clearly and avoid using slang.
6. Give the other person time to think, reply and/or take notes.
7. Where appropriate, show you are listening by saying 'uh-huh', 'yes, I see', and so on.
8. Make a note of important details (for example, quantities, dates, prices and reference numbers) and run through them at the end of the conversation to make sure you wrote them down correctly.
9. Give your details so you can be contacted by telephone or post.
10. Finish the call appropriately (for example, say 'thanks' or 'look forward to seeing you on Friday'), using the other person's name if possible.

Making presentations

Much of the work you carry out for your GNVQ, and many of the activities in this book, ask you to make oral presentations. You need certain skills to give a good business presentation, and this section will help you.

For more on making presentations, see page 89.

Preparing the room

When you are going to make a presentation, get to the room early (before your audience) so that you can check everything is ready.

Run through the following checklist.
- Is the room set out the way you want?
- Are there enough chairs? Too many chairs?
- Can everyone see the overhead projector (OHP)?
- Is the OHP working?
- Is there a table for you?
- Do you need marker pens and a board cleaner? If so, have you got them?

Toolkit

Preparing yourself

Always dress suitably when you're giving a business presentation. Make sure that your clothes are neat and tidy. This might seem unimportant, but customers will look at you as the representative of your company.

Stand up straight and look at your audience. It can be difficult to hear someone who is looking down all the time. Try it with your friends and see how quickly your voice is lost if you look down.

Planning what to say

Your presentation needs to have a clear structure. You should always start by telling people who you are and why you are there. You should know for how long you are going to talk, and whether or not you want people to ask questions as you go along or at the end.

A timetable is a useful way to remind yourself of your plan. For example, the plan for a twenty-minute presentation to market a new soft drink might look like the one on the left.

Getting your message across

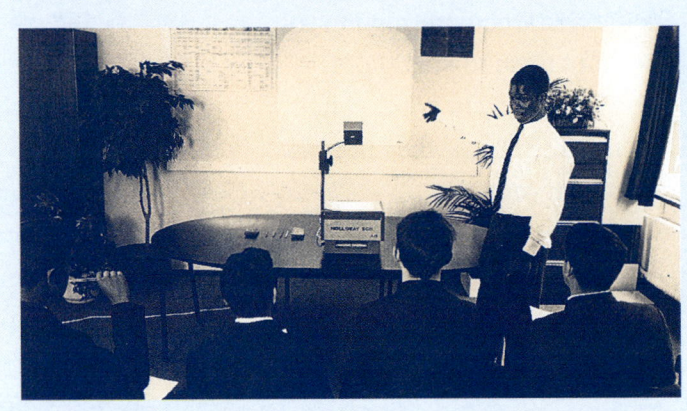

You should speak very clearly, and loudly enough for the people at the back of the room to hear you. Reading from notes muffles your voice and limits eye contact, so make sure you know what you are going to say in advance. If you want something to remind you, write key words or sentences on small cards and keep them next to you.

Practise your presentation before you actually give it. Try timing your talk as well – sometimes it's surprising how long or short a time it takes. If you practise in front of a mirror, you will get an idea of what the audience will see. This may help you avoid fidgeting, using mannerisms, or doing things that will stop your audience concentrating on what you are saying.

Try to give your audience something to look at. Overhead transparencies are a good idea, as you can prepare them in advance. If you use overhead transparency pens, avoid red and green – they are difficult to see. If there isn't an overhead projector, write on the whiteboard or blackboard. Or you may be able to borrow a flip chart with large sheets of paper. Again, practise in advance to make sure that you make your letters large enough for everyone to see, and spell all the words correctly.

PLAN FOR TALK

- **2 minutes — Introduction**
  "Good morning/afternoon. My name is... I'm here to tell you about the new..... drink."

- **5 minutes — Why a new drink?**
  "This drink is special because....."

- **1 minute — What does it look like?**
  Show the drink with its packaging

- **5 minutes — Why should you buy this drink?**
  An OHT showing:
  - price
  - flavour
  - availability
  - who will like it

- **2 minutes — Conclusion**
  "Thank you for coming here today. This is to remind you that we have been talking about ...."

- **5 minutes — Questions**
  "Has anyone any questions they would like to ask?"

Communication

Body language

For more on body language, see page 97.

Body language is the term used for the ways our bodies send messages – messages which may make people believe, or not believe, what our words are saying.

The body can send messages in many ways; for example, through:

- the eyes – making eye contact shows the person you're talking to that you're listening
- the face – your facial expression can show your attitude to an idea, argument or suggestion
- gestures with the head, arms and legs, and hands – to show agreement or disagreement, anger or calm, certainty or doubt, enthusiasm or boredom. For example, folding your arms can hold people at a distance, while opening your arms can show welcome
- posture – for example, leaning forward shows you're interested
- position in relation to others – for example, sitting close to people can show that you're comfortable with their views or feelings.

With experience, body language can be a useful way to make your views clear. But take care your body doesn't tell a story you don't want told.

Just by looking at the people in these three different examples, can you guess what each of them is thinking in each case?

Toolkit

Writing skills

It's not always possible, or convenient, to explain something to someone face-to-face or over the telephone. If this is the case, you need to write to them.

Formal letters

All letters apart from those we send to family and friends are **formal letters**. Here are some things to think about when you write a formal letter.

Reference number – if there is one, quote the reference number from their letter to you and give them yours. This can help with filing and finding letters.

Recipient's name and address – to make it clear to whom you're sending the letter.

Date of writing in full, including the word for the month, in the order day-month-year.

Greeting – 'Dear ....'. Use the person's name if possible.

Introductory sentence or paragraph – should expand on the title and prepare the reader for the rest of the letter.

The concluding paragraph – this may be a single sentence that sums up what you will do, or would like the other person to do.

The subscription – a polite, formal phrase before the signature. If the letter is written to a named person, use 'Yours sincerely'. Otherwise, write 'Yours faithfully'.

Your ref: 289/FO1

24 Headley Road
Rainford
Surrey GU14 6QT

Mr J Timms
Personnel Manager
Atherton Systems Ltd.
Bridge Street
Rainford
Surrey GU13 2JL

20 June 1995

Dear Mr Timms

Application for the post of Junior Finance Officer

I would like to apply for the post of Junior Finance Officer at Atherton Systems advertised in the Evening Echo on 16 June 1995.

I am currently a student at St Bartholomew's School in Rainford, studying for Foundation GNVQ in Business and GCSEs in Computer Studies and Technology. I already have three GCSEs, as you can see from the enclosed CV.

I am leaving college in September and hope to work in an office as I enjoy working with people and would like to make the most of my business skills. I have already spent time on work experience in local offices, as well as having a part-time job in a local supermarket.

I am available for interview at any time and hope to hear from you in the near future.

Yours sincerely

Rachel Vaughan

Rachel Vaughan

Your address – should be clear and written in full (include your postcode, and write 'Road', not 'Rd').

Title – a short heading that explains what the letter's about; for example, a job. pplication or a letter of complaint.

The body of the letter – the main points, with detail. The number of paragraphs you include will depend on how complicated the subject.

The signature – even if this is legible, you should print your name underneath.

Always write as accurately and as clearly as possible. Don't be 'chatty', but keep to words you can use confidently. If you write the letter on a computer, do a spell check.

Collect a range of formal letters to compare them. If you think any of the information in them might be private, blank it out so that people can't read it.

Communication

Memoranda (memos)

Memoranda (shortened to 'memos' by most people) are a way to communicate quickly and easily within organisations.

For example, on 12 June 1995 John Timms, Personnel Manager at Atherton Systems Ltd., sent this memo to Freda Smith, the Finance Manager, about the job for which Rachel Vaughan applied. He used one of the company's blank memos.

MEMO

atherton**SYSTEMS** ltd.

internal memorandum

From: John Timms   Date: 12 June 1995
To: Freda Smith
Subject: Finance Officer vacancy

I confirm that an advertisement for the vacant post of Junior Finance Officer in your office will appear in the Evening Echo for 16 June.

I have the job description and person specification agreed with you and will prepare a short-list of candidates for your comments on 28th June.

Interview date: 5 July, 2.00 – 5.00, Room 7

J.T.

— The headed memo form shows that it is an Atherton Systems internal memo.

— The form prompts Mr Timms to supply the basic information: from whom, to whom, when, about what. This provides a record for filing.

— The blank memo has enough space for a short message. It encourages people to be brief, and give the facts in plain language and simple style.

— Initialling the memo gives a personal touch, and also confirms it is genuine.

Think how much longer it would have taken John Timms to write a letter.

Toolkit

BUSINESSES IN CAPSTONE

Capstone is a very old town with lots of thatched houses and historical things to see. The photograph here shows one of the streets in the town where lots of visitors stay. People come to Capstone because it is peaceful and pretty, and it is just 1 mile from the sea so lots of families come here on holiday.

Most of the businesses in Capstone are small local businesses like family shops, bed and breakfasts and farms. I talked to 30 people who live in the town to see what type of businesses they work in. This bar chart shows what I found out.

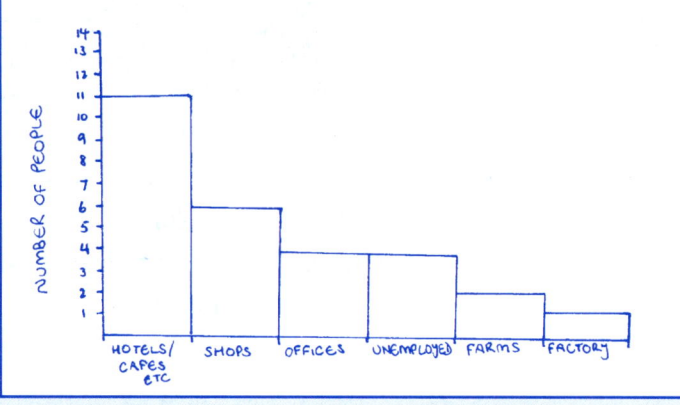

This student has used images to make her report clearer

For more on bar charts and pictograms, see page 18.

Using images

Images are pictures – such as bar charts, flow charts, pictograms and photographs – which can help make written communication clearer.

Helpful hints

- Don't use images just to make your work prettier – use them to help you communicate. Make sure that the image you use is appropriate – you might be tempted to use a striking image when it's not actually relevant.
- Whenever you make an important point in writing or speech, ask yourself whether you could make your point clearer by including an image.

Simple reports

Your reports shouldn't be mystery tours with surprising endings – they should follow clear, easy-to-follow paths, pointing to the end from the start.

Try using the following structure for your reports.

- Title page, including the report title, your name and date.
- Terms of reference – what you were asked to do. Include this so you can refer back to it when writing your conclusions.
- Methods used – reading, observing, interviewing and so on.
- Findings – the facts, figures and views. You might present these in a variety of ways, including graphs and pictograms.
- Conclusions – what do your findings tell you? For instance, if you interviewed shoppers and found that the majority worried about traffic problems in the High Street, you might conclude that a pedestrian precinct would be popular.
- Sources – include a list of the books and periodicals you referred to, and the people and organisations you talked to. Arrange them in sections, in alphabetical order.

Use words you're sure you understand and write in a straightforward style. You're usually expected to be impersonal. For instance, a report on crime prevention in hotels would probably read:

"The two porters, James Merton and William Grant, were interviewed about their views on preventing pilfering…"

not

"Jim and Bill told me what they'd do to catch the thieves on the staff."

Application of Number and Information Technology

As well as being able to communicate well with people, you need to be able to use numbers and computers when working in business. This is why Foundation GNVQ Business includes core skills units in Application of Number (maths) and Information Technology (using computers).

This section includes some information, advice and activities which might help you on your way.

Percentages

It is very important to remember that a **percentage** is just a particular type of **fraction**.

ninths $\frac{75}{99}$ quarters $\frac{27}{39}$ $\frac{135}{367}$ tenths $\frac{200}{365}$ half $3/7$

$3.04 = 3\frac{4}{100}$ $0.78 = \frac{78}{100}$

- **Fractions** can have **any** whole number as a **denominator** (bottom number). This means there are many different types of fraction.

- **Decimal fractions** can only have powers of **10** as denominators (tenths, hundredths, thousandths and so on), so we can put them in columns to match whole numbers. We use the decimal point to show where the whole numbers stop and the fractions start.

- Percentages are fractions out of 100.
- Per cent means 'for each hundred' or 'out of a hundred'.

We use a special sign as a quick way of writing per cent – %. This means the same as /100.

So...

$7\% = \frac{7}{100}$ $26\% = \frac{26}{100}$ $100\% = \frac{100}{100} = 1$

Watch out! 100% does not mean 100.

To **use** a percentage we need to write it as a fraction.

Example

To find 6% of £40, change 6% to its fraction form and multiply by £40.

$6\% \text{ of } £40 = \frac{6}{100} \times 40 = £2.40$

Using a calculator:

`6 ÷ 1 0 0 x 4 0 = 2 . 4`

We write **money** with **two** numbers after the decimal point to represent the pence, so 2.4 becomes £2.40.

Toolkit

For more on VAT, see page 50.

VAT

In business, people often need to work out VAT (Value Added Tax) which is given as a percentage.

Example

If you need to add VAT to £65 and the rate of VAT is 17.5%, change 17.5% to its fraction form then multiply by £65.

$$17.5\% \text{ of } £65 = \frac{17.5}{100} \times 65 = £11.375 = £11.38$$

Using a calculator:

`17.5 ÷ 100 x 65 = 11.375`

This gives you too many decimal places, so you need to **round** the answer to the nearest penny, giving you £11.38.

This is the amount of VAT. Add this to the original price to get the total:

$$£65 + VAT = £65 + £11.38 = £76.38$$

Rounding numbers
- If a decimal is exactly halfway (or more than halfway) between two numbers, you should round it up to the next penny. So £11.375 becomes £11.38.
- If a decimal is less than halfway between two numbers, you should round it down to the penny below. So £6.342 becomes £6.34.

For more on discounts, see page 50.

Discounts

A discount is an amount taken off the total cost of something; for example, a 20% discount means there is 20% off the price.

To find a 20% discount, you need to find 20% of the price and then take the answer away from the original amount.

Example

A tennis racket originally cost £35, but now has a discount of 20% in the sale. To find out the discount and the new sale price of the tennis racket, you need to find 20% of £35:

$$20\% \text{ of } £35 = \frac{20}{100} \times 35 = £7$$

Using a calculator:

`20 ÷ 100 x 35 = 7`

So to find the racket's new selling price, take £7 from the original price of £35:

$$£35 - £7 = £28$$

Application of Number and Information Technology

Activity
Using percentages

'With a 40% discount?'

'Plus 17.5% VAT?'

Find out the answers to the following questions using percentages.

1 a John gets a garage bill for £164 plus VAT at 17.5%. How much VAT does he have to pay?
   b What is the total garage bill?

2 Gita gets a bill for herself and her friend's meal which reads £36.40. The restaurant adds a further 10% for service. What is the total bill including service?

3 a Jaswinder is to pay £420 for her holiday. If she pays by 28 February she is allowed a 5% reduction. How much would this reduction be?
   b How much would she have to pay if she paid on 27 February?

4 A pair of trainers is marked '10% off marked price'. If the marked price is £58.98, what is the reduced price?

5 A college refectory served 2340 meals in the first week in May. In the following week the number of meals dropped by 15%. How many meals did it serve during the second week?

6 Look at the following invoice. Find out the figures for total price, total cost, discount, sub total, VAT and net payable.

Invoice No.		Unit price £0.00	Total price £0.00
Quantity	Description	3.49	£
		1.99	£
2	M1475 Reinforcements		
4	M-1874		
		Total cost	£
		Discount 10%	£
		Sub total	£
		Add VAT 17.5%	£
		Net payable	£

See page 31 for the answers.

17

Toolkit

Pictorial presentation

It is often useful to include graphs and charts in your work. They can give a good picture of data, making it easier to see the general result. Remember, because they are pictures they often do not provide detailed information. For detail, you should look at the original information.

During your GNVQ you will use:

Bar charts
- each bar is the same width
- each bar should be labelled
- the height of the bar shows 'how many', the frequency
- one axis has a scale; the other has labels
- bar charts can be horizontal or vertical

Pictograms
- also known as pictographs
- use symbols (pictures) rather than bars
- all pictures should be the same size
- pictures are chosen to emphasise the topic

Bar charts

Bar charts, or graphs, can be drawn with the bars horizontal or with the bars vertical. Vertical bar charts are the most common.

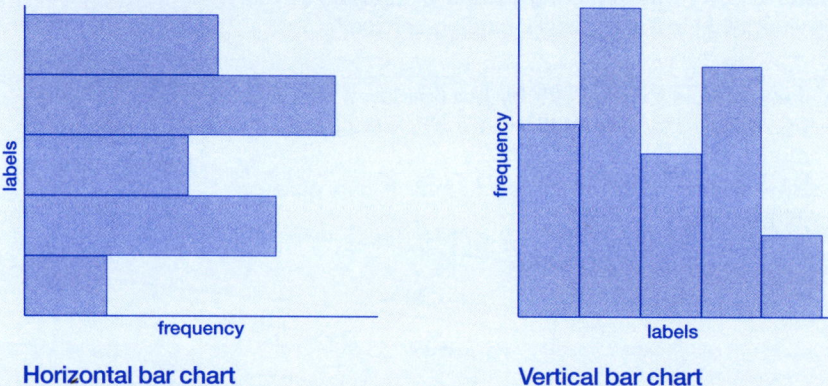

Horizontal bar chart **Vertical bar chart**

The axis for frequency must be to **scale** – evenly spaced. The main decision you have to make is **what scale to use**.

Look at the frequency information and, if you are drawing your chart by hand, the number of squares on your graph paper. Choose a scale which will fit the paper well. Be careful not to choose a difficult scale – keep to 2's, 5's, 10's, 20's, 25's, 50's, 100's. Avoid 3's and other awkward numbers.

Drawing a bar chart

Having decided on the scale for your frequency, you need to draw bars to the correct height. Make sure you understand the meaning of your scale and the smaller parts of it; for example, what does 0.5 cm show on your graph?

Each bar must be the **same width**. You can leave gaps between the bars if you wish, or you can keep them next to each other. Make the graph fit on the page and give it a title.

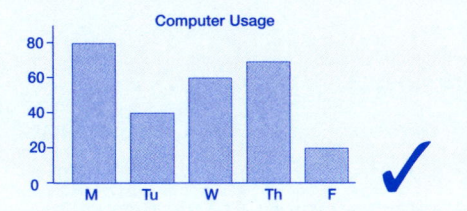

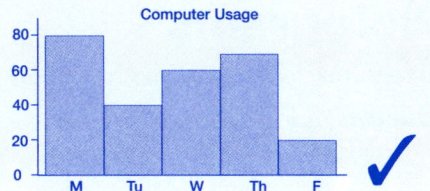

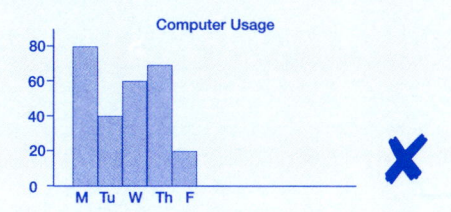

Application of Number and Information Technology

The height of each bar should match its 'frequency' (how many times it occurs). There is no need to put the bars in order of size.

Reading a bar chart

Having drawn the graph, you can use it to find out information.

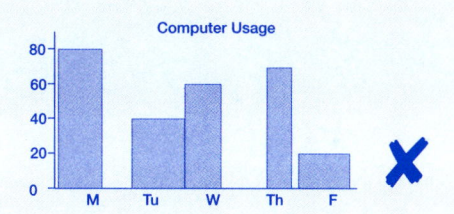

Example

The following table shows the weekly takings of a small sweet shop over one week:

Day	Takings (£)
Mon	40
Tue	30
Wed	45
Thur	10
Fri	30
Sat	50

A bar chart showing this information might look like this:

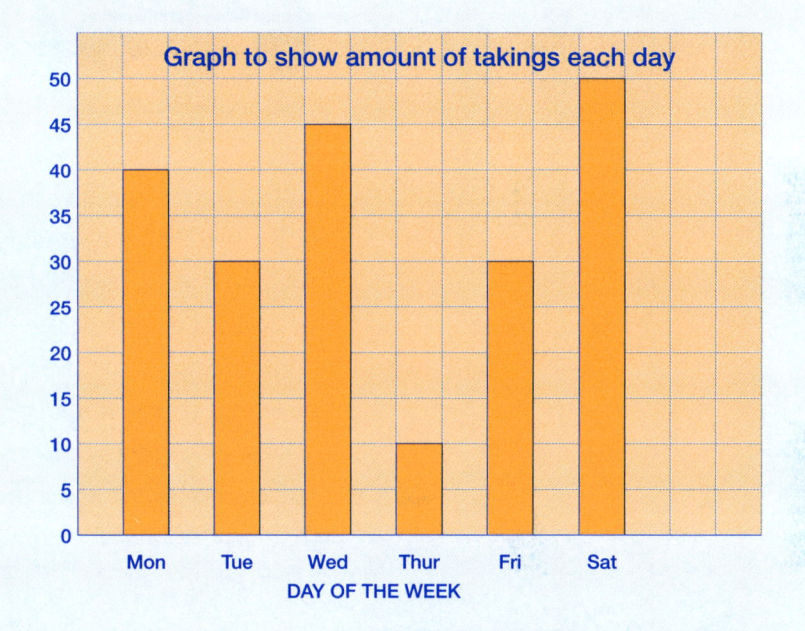

Which day appears to be the most popular?

Which day is most likely to be half-day closing?

See page 31 for the answers.

Activity

Reading graphs

Mr Boghal runs a small supermarket. He writes down his takings (to the nearest £10) for each day in one week:

Day	Mon	Tue	Wed	Thur	Fri	Sat
Takings	£300	£500	£250	£650	£500	£900

Use squared paper to draw a bar chart showing the shop's daily takings.

Look at your graph and answer these questions:

1. Which day is the least popular?
2. Which day has the greatest takings?
3. Which two days had the same takings?

See page 31 for the answers.

Toolkit

Pictograms

Pictograms are graphs which use pictures to make a point clearly. For example:

- if your topic is cigarette smoking, you might use pictures of cigarettes
- if your topic is the number killed in a war, you might use pictures of crosses or coffins
- if your topic is traffic, you might use pictures of cars, lorries or buses.

Note: even if you use different pictures in the same graph, each picture must be the same size.

To save time and effort we usually let each picture represent more than 1. For example:

might represent 200 buses    might represent less than 200 buses    might represent 1000 houses

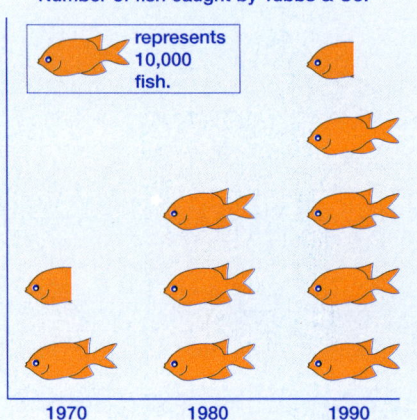

One of the problems with pictograms is that it is difficult to show the difference between similar numbers, for example 691 buses and 695 buses. You could show part of a bus to show less than 200 buses, but you couldn't show detailed differences.

The pictogram on the left shows the increase in number of fish caught over a 20-year period.

This doesn't show exactly how many fish Tubbs & Co caught each year – you can't tell how many the 'part fish' represents. The important thing is that it shows that the number of fish being caught is **increasing quickly**.

Number of fish caught by Tubbs & Co.

represents 10,000 fish.

1970   1980   1990

Activity
Using pictograms

1 Martian Oil Field produced the following amounts of oil between 1977 and 1981:

   1977   15,000 litres
   1978   26,000 litres
   1979   30,000 litres
   1980   44,000 litres
   1981   60,500 litres

The manager of the oil field produced a report to show how the company was growing. Draw a pictogram for the manager to include in the report. Let one barrel represent 10,000 litres.

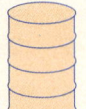

2 The council of Swan Village drew the pictogram below to show how the population of the village was growing.
   Use the pictogram to answer the following questions:
   a What was the approximate population of Swan Village in 1950?
   b What was the approximate increase in the population between 1950 and 1990?
   c What was the approximate population of Swan Village in 1990?

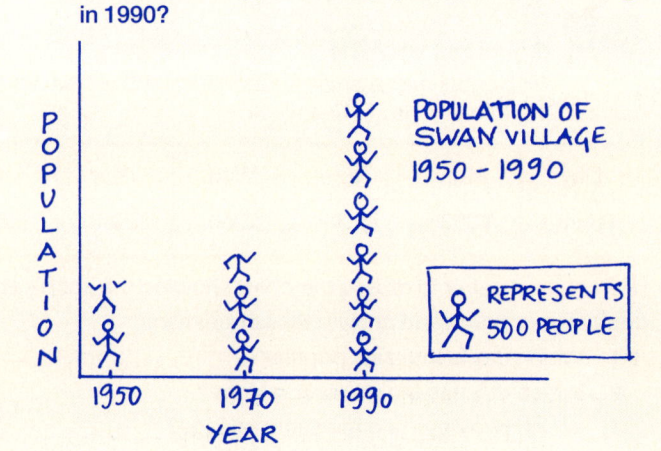

POPULATION OF SWAN VILLAGE 1950 – 1990

REPRESENTS 500 PEOPLE

1950   1970   1990
YEAR

See page 31 for the answers.

Application of Number and Information Technology

Measure

In Britain, we currently use two systems of measurement – the Imperial System and the Metric System.

Systems of measurement

The **Imperial System** has been used in Britain for many years. It includes different systems for **weight**, **length** and **capacity** (measuring liquids and volumes) developed a long time ago. For example, the measurement of one foot was about the length of a man's foot, and a yard about one stride! We still use some of these measures, even though we have 'gone metric'.

The **Metric System** was introduced in Britain fairly recently. It is widely used in the rest of Europe. Each metric measure uses a number system based on **thousands**. There is a base unit for each type of measurement (the metre for length, the gram for weight, and the litre for capacity). Each of these can be broken down into 1000 small pieces (millimetres, milligrams and millilitres), or 1000 can be joined together to make a larger measurement (kilometre, kilogram and kilolitre). Because the millimetre (mm) and millilitre (ml) are very small, we also use the centimetre (10 mm) and the centilitre (10 ml).

The metric system was designed to link different units:

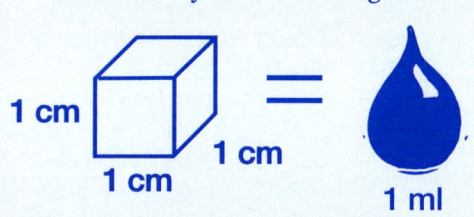

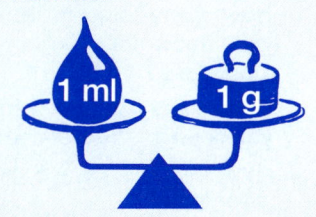

1 cubic centimetre of water has a volume of 1 millilitre and weighs 1 gram

Look out for imperial and metric measures in shops:

- What is the normal weight of a bag of sugar or a bag of flour?
- How do you buy your milk?
- Would you ask your grocer for a pound of apples or a kilo of apples?
- Do we buy petrol by the litre or by the gallon?

Which is measured using the Metric System – beer or wine?

Beer is measured in **pints**

Wine is measured in **centilitres**

Metric and imperial

The Imperial System

Length

12 inches = 1 foot (12" = 1')
3 feet = 1 yard (3' = 1 yd)
1760 yards = 1 mile

Weight

16 ounces = 1 pound (16 oz = 1 lb)
14 pounds = 1 stone (14 lb = 1 st)
112 pounds = 1 hundredweight (112 lb = 1 cwt)
20 hundredweight = 1 ton (20 cwt = 1 t)

Capacity

20 fluid ounces = 1 pint (20 fl oz = 1 pt)
2 pints = 1 quart (2 pt = 1 qt)
8 pints = 1 gallon (8 pt = 1 gal)

Temperature

Measured in degrees Fahrenheit (°F)
Water freezes at 32°F
Water boils at 212°F

Toolkit

The Metric System

Length
1000 millimetres = 1 metre
(1000 mm = 1 m)
1000 metres = 1 kilometre
(1000 m = 1 km)
10 millimetres = 1 centimetre
(10 mm = 1 cm)
100 centimetres = 1 metre
(100 cm = 1 m)

Weight
1000 milligrams = 1 gram
(1000 mg = 1 g)
1000 grams = 1 kilogram
(1000 g = 1 kg)
1000 kilograms = 1 tonne
(1000 kg = 1 t)

Capacity
1000 millilitres = 1 litre
(1000 ml = 1 l)
(the kilolitre is not often used)
10 millilitres = 1 centilitre
(10 ml = 1 cl)
100 centilitres = 1 litres
(100 cl = 1 l)

Temperature
Measured in degrees Celsius or Centigrade (°C)
Water freezes at 0°C
Water boils at 100°C

Changing between metric and imperial

Approximately:
- 2.5 cm = 1 inch
- 30 cm = 1 foot
- 1 metre = 39 inches = 1 yard 3 inches
- 8 kilometres = 5 miles
- 1 kilogram = 2.2 pounds (lb)
- 1 litre = 1.75 pints

To change:
- °F to °C, subtract 32, multiply by 5 and divide by 9
- °C to °F, multiply by 9, divide by 5, and add 32.

Activity
Using measurements

You are an administrative officer at a local sports hall. You have been set the task of finding the cost of revarnishing and marking lines on the floor.

The sports hall measures 15 metres by 28 metres.

1. Estimate the amount of varnish needed for the floor and the cost of the varnish.

a What is the area of the sports hall floor?
b How many litres of varnish will you need for a normal coat (undiluted)?
c How many litres of varnish will you need for the first coat?
d How many litres will you need altogether?
e How much will this cost?

Super Varnish
- Each litre covers 15 square metres.
- The first coat must be diluted with water in the ratio 3:1 (3 parts varnish to 1 part water)
- Then give 2 more coats for a superb finish!
- Allow 4 hours between coats.

Only £1.20 per litre

Varnish

	Number of litres	Cost per litre	Cost per court
1st coat		£1.20	
2nd coat		£1.20	
3rd coat		£1.20	
		Total cost	

Lines

	Number of metres	Number of courts	Cost per metre	Cost per court
5-a-side		1	£0.05	
Basketball		1	£0.05	
Badminton		4	£0.05	
			Total cost	

2. Find out the cost of marking lines on the floor. The floor is to be marked with a five-a-side football pitch, a basketball court and four badminton courts. You may need to visit a sports hall to find out how this is done.

a Find out the sizes of these pitches/courts and what lines need to be drawn. The cost of marking the lines is given as 5 pence per metre.
b Estimate how many metres of lines are likely to be needed. How much would this cost? For circles, estimate the circumference (distance round the edge) by multiplying the diameter (distance across the middle of the circle) by 3.
c Draw a sketch of the sports hall showing roughly how the lines will be drawn.
d Draw a scale drawing of the sports hall with the lines drawn, using a scale of 1 centimetre representing 1 metre. Measure the lengths of the lines you have drawn.

3. Produce a short report including your working out, your costing, your sketch and scale drawings and the tables on the left completed. You might find a spreadsheet helpful when working out total costs.

See page 31 for the answers.

Application of Number and Information Technology

Paper

Businesses use a great deal of paper. Most will be of standard 'International Paper Size' – the most common is called the 'A' Series. This includes:

- A0 paper, which has an area of 1 square metre. It measures 841 mm x 1189 mm (to the nearest millimetre)
- A1 paper, which is half the size of A0
- A2 paper, which is half the size of A1; and so on.

The diagram below shows the relative sizes of paper from A0 down to A6 size, although there are also smaller sizes. Probably the most common size for letters is A4, which measures 210 mm x 297 mm.

Paper is usually bought in reams (500 sheets) or quires (25 sheets).

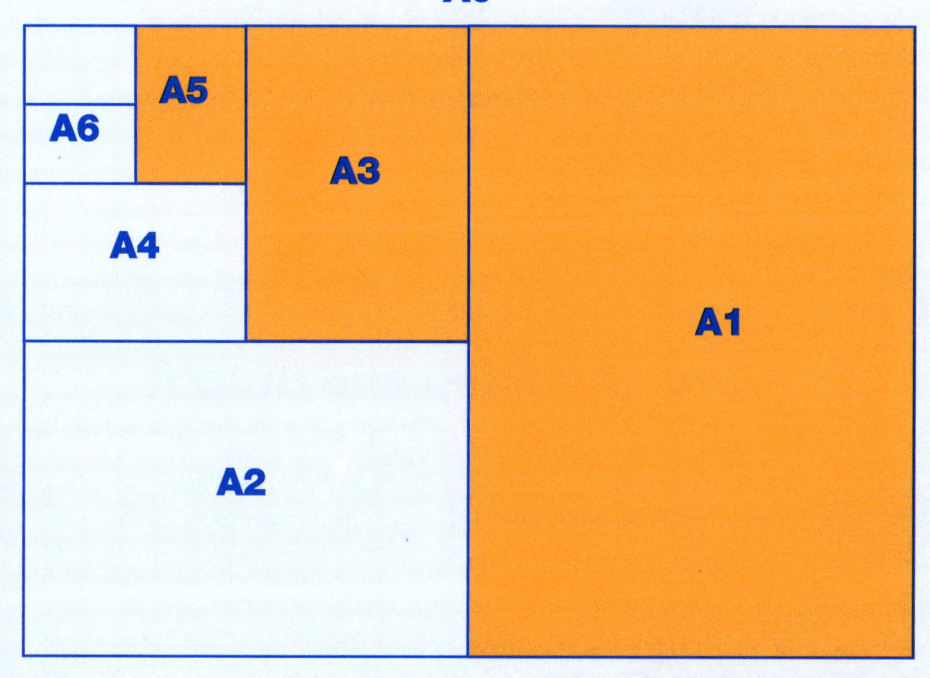

	Size in mm
A0	841 X 1189
A1	594 X 841
A2	420 X 594
A3	297 X 420
A4	210 X 297
A5	148 X 210
A6	105 X 148
A7	74 X 105
A8	52 X 74
A9	37 X 52

Toolkit

Conversion

If you need to change from one unit of measurement to another (for example, from litres to gallons), you can use:
- a conversion factor
- a conversion table
- a conversion chart or graph.

Conversion factors

A **conversion factor** is useful if you have only one or two calculations to do and you're not going to need to do them very often.

Example

- the conversion factor to change litres to gallons is 0.22
- the conversion factor to change gallons to litres is 4.546

This means that **1 litre is 0.22 gallons**, and there are **4.546 litres in 1 gallon**.

- to change litres to gallons you need to multiply by 0.22
- to change gallons to litres you multiply by 4.546

So if you buy 30 litres of petrol you are buying:

30 x 0.22 gallons of petrol = 6.6 gallons

If you convert measurements only occasionally, you will probably use a conversion factor

Conversion tables and graphs

Conversion tables and graphs are useful if you have to change measurements from one unit to another regularly.

With a **conversion table**, the numbers are worked out once, using the conversion factor, and the answers are put in the table. This means that you can read the table instead of working out the answers each time.

A conversion table for gallons and litres might look like this:

Gallons		Litres
0.220	1	4.546
0.440	2	9.092
0.660	3	13.638
0.880	4	18.184
1.101	5	22.730

If you convert measurements regularly, you will probably use a conversion table or graph

You can read a conversion table in two ways:
- read the middle column as gallons and the right-hand column as litres; or
- read the middle column as litres and the left-hand column as gallons.

Application of Number and Information Technology

The conversion table can be designed to go as high as you think you might need. Each of the numbers in the table can be rounded to the degree of accuracy you need; for example:

1 gallon = 4.546 litres = 4.5 litres

However, a conversion table does not answer all problems – could you use the table on page 24 to change 3.5 gallons to litres?

To do this, it might be useful to draw a **conversion graph or chart**. Using the answers already worked out for the conversion table, you can plot **three** useful points on a graph:

- 0 litres = 0.0 gallons
- 10 litres = 2.2 gallons
- 20 litres = 4.4 gallons.

By joining these points together to give a straight line, you can read all other conversions from this graph, as shown below.

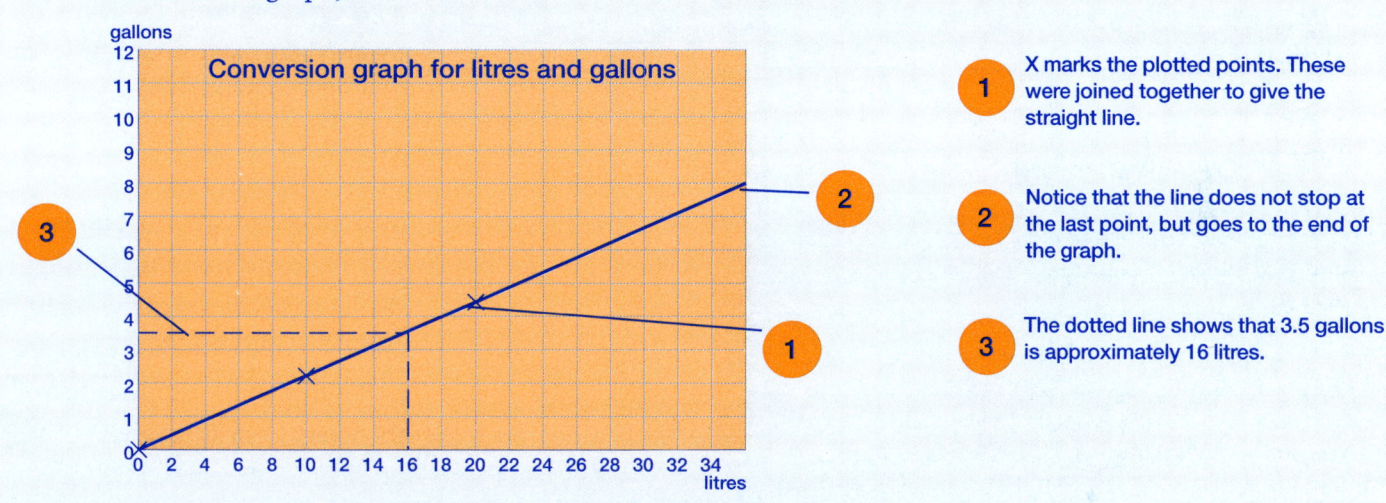

Conversion graph for litres and gallons

1. X marks the plotted points. These were joined together to give the straight line.

2. Notice that the line does not stop at the last point, but goes to the end of the graph.

3. The dotted line shows that 3.5 gallons is approximately 16 litres.

A conversion graph is often not as accurate as using a conversion factor or conversion table (using the conversion factor, 3.5 gallons = 15.911 litres), but it is a quick way to change between units.

Activity
Conversion graphs

1. Draw the graph converting litres to gallons for yourself. Use your graph to answer these questions.
    a. How many litres are there in 10 gallons?
    b. How many gallons are there in 25 litres?
    c. Information about a new car gives the petrol tank capacity as 34 litres. If petrol costs 55.9 pence per litre, how much would it cost to fill the petrol tank?
    d. How many gallons does the tank hold?
    e. The information also says that the car is economical, and can travel 50 miles per gallon (at 50 mph). How far can the car travel on 1 tank of petrol?
    f. How much does this cost per mile?

2. Mr and Mrs James see this advertisement for bedroom carpet, and decide to buy 15 square metres.

ST★R BUY
Joe's Carpets
Bedroom Carpet
only
£3.99 a sq yard
3 or 4 metres wide

The sign shows that carpets are measured in square metres, but priced by the square yard. Joe has a conversion graph on the wall to convert square metres to square yards. He used the following values to draw his graph:

Square metres	Square yards
0	0
10	12
20	24
30	36

Use these values to draw Joe's conversion graph.

a. From the graph, how many square yards will Mr and Mrs James be charged for?
b. How much will they pay for their carpet?

See page 31 for the answers.

Toolkit

Using information technology

Computers are very good at dealing with numbers and producing graphs. It is important that we know how to produce graphs by hand, but a large business would always use IT to produce well-finished graphs or charts.

To produce a graph or chart on the computer, you have to begin with a spreadsheet or database.

For more about using spreadsheets, see page 57.

Using a spreadsheet

The following information is **generally** true, but you must learn how to use the spreadsheet package you have at school or college as they are all slightly different.

When you use a spreadsheet or database, you put all the information into a table like the one below. These are the sales figures sent to head office by a grocery shop with branches in Swan Village and in Queenstown. The table shows the amount (in £) taken by different sections of the stores in one week.

Each piece of information is placed in a **cell**, described using the letter at the top of the column and the number at the beginning of the row. In the example here, the word 'Item' is in cell A1. The number 5600 is in cell C2.

GNVQ Worksheet

A1 × ✓ Item

	A	B	C	D
1	Item	Swan Village	Queenstown	
2	Tins & packets	200	5600	
3	Fresh fruit/veg	148	2100	
4	Meat/fish	120	2340	
5	Dairy	84	960	
6	Other	24	520	
7				
8				
9				

Producing graphs

By using the graph option in the spreadsheet or database package, you can produce charts like these:

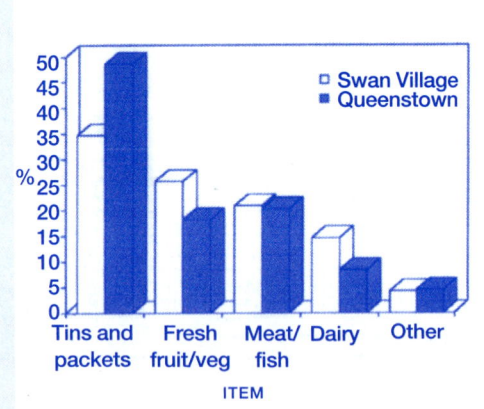

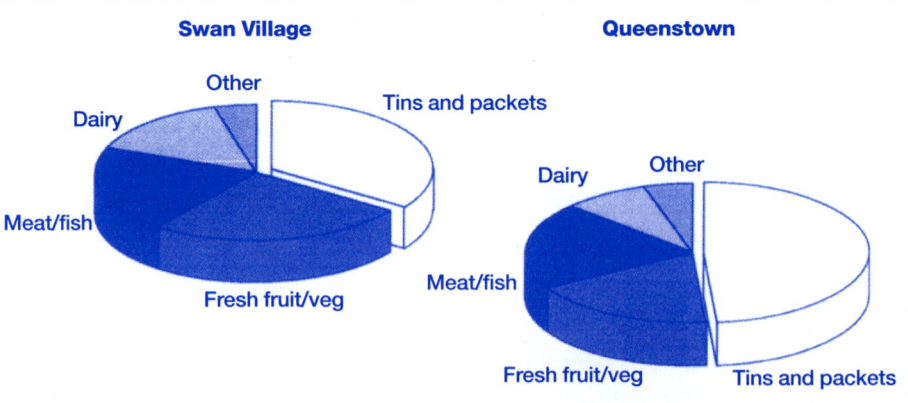

For the bar chart and pie chart, the information has been changed to percentages. You can do this by using a calculator and typing in the answers, but it is better to use the power of the spreadsheet by putting in a formula.

Application of Number and Information Technology

	A	B	C	D	E	F
1	Item	Swan Village	Queenstown			
2	Tins & packets	200	5600			
3	Fresh fruit/veg	148	2100			
4	Meat/fish	120	2340			
5	Dairy	84	960			
6	Other	24	520			
7		← B7				
8						
9						
10						

Step 1: working out totals

The total number of sales for Swan Village should go in cell B7. To do this, you need to select B7, then enter a formula.

The formula might look like this:

=B2+B3+B4+B5+B6

or like this:

=SUM(B2:B6)

This should give a total of 576.

Repeat this process for Queenstown. You should get a total of 11,520.

Step 2: working out percentages

The percentage of Swan Village's total sales that came from tins and packets should go in cell D2. This will be:

$^{200}/_{576}$ x 100 (200 as a percentage of the total number of sales – 576)

The formula might look like this:

=B2/B7*100

Notice that / is used to divide and * is used to multiply, and that we use B7 rather than the number 576.

The answer is 34.722222. If you don't need this number of decimal places, you can **format** the cell to give whole numbers only. This will give you the answer 35%.

If you work out percentages for all the other amounts from Swan Village, and repeat the process for Queenstown, your spreadsheet should look something like this:

	A	B	C	D	E	F
1	Item	Swan Village	Queenstown	Percent 1	Percent 2	
2	Tins & packets	200	5600	35	49	
3	Fresh fruit/veg	148	2100	26	18	
4	Meat/fish	120	2340	21	20	
5	Dairy	84	960	15	8	
6	Other	24	520	4	5	
7	Total	576	11520			
8						
9						
10						

The percent columns should always add up to approximately 100%. (You might get 99% or 101% if figures are rounded up or down.)

Toolkit

Activity
Using a spreadsheet

Now use a spreadsheet package to work through these steps yourself.

1. Enter the information about sales figures in Swan Village and Queenstown into a spreadsheet package, making sure that each piece of information is in a cell.
2. Work out total sales for Swan Village and Queenstown using a formula (see Step 1).
3. Work out the percentages of different types of sales in Swan Village and Queenstown (see Step 2).
4. Now use the graph function to produce a bar chart using Percent 1 and Percent 2. Your chart should look like the one on page 26.

Safety first!

It is important to take safety into account when using IT equipment. How would you do things differently to the person below?

Position screen to avoid reflections.

Store discs away from heat and electrical equipment.

Keep drinks away from equipment.

Keep cables tidy. Make sure cables are connected properly.

Application of Number and Information Technology

The mean, the mode and the range

The mean

This is the best-known average, also known as the **arithmetic mean**.

To help you understand, imagine six people have money, as shown on the right.

At the moment, the money isn't shared out equally – some people have more than others! Calculating the mean is like finding out how much each would have if the money was shared out equally. The total amount of money must stay the same.

To work this out they could put all their money on the table and then share it out. In our example, the total amount of money would be:

£6 + £5 + £3 + £2 + £1 + £1 = **£18**

Sharing this out equally between the six of them would give each one:

£18 ÷ 6 = **£3 each**

£3 is the mean.

> To find the mean, find the total, then divide it by the number of pieces of data. When you find the mean, always use every piece of data.

> **Note:**
> - the mean doesn't have to be one of the original numbers
> - the mean doesn't have to be a whole number – even when you're talking about people!

Example

To find the mean of £34, £56, £65, £72, £84:
- find the total – £34 + £56 + £65 + £72 + £84 = £311
- divide it by the number of pieces of data – £311 ÷ 5 = £62.2 = £62.20

The mode

This is the simplest average to 'work out'.

The mode is the most popular or most frequent figure – the value that crops up most often.

Example

On 15 days in November, 'Brollys' the umbrella shop sold this many umbrellas:

8, 6, 8, 7, 6, 8, 7, 5, 8, 6, 7, 8, 8, 7, 8

From these figures you can draw a **frequency table** – a table showing how often Brollys sold a particular number of umbrellas a day.

Toolkit

A quick way to do this is to **tally** the data – for each number put a mark. To help keep track (especially for large numbers) we group marks into fives, as shown on the left. This is called a '5-barred gate' – the fifth mark is put across the other 4 to 'tie' them together.

From our numbers, we get:

Data	Tally	Frequency
5	I	1
6	III	3
7	IIII	4
8	IIII II	7

We can see that, on these 15 days in November, Brollys most frequently sold 8 umbrellas. We therefore say that the **modal number** sold is 8 umbrellas.

The range

The **range** of a set of numbers is the difference between the largest and the smallest.

So... the range of 3, 8, 6, 9, 2, 7 = 9 – 2 = 7

To find the range of a set of numbers, simply look for the largest value and the smallest value, and work out the difference.

Look again at the number of umbrellas Brollys sold on 15 days in November:

8, 6, 8, 7, 6, 8, 7, 5, 8, 6, 7, 8, 8, 7, 8

The range is 8 – 5 = 3

Activity
Mean, mode and range

Forget-me-not the florists sells both red and white roses. During one week it sold the following numbers:

	Mon	Tue	Wed	Thur	Fri	Sat
Red	5	3	4	3	2	13
White	5	5	5	4	5	6

1 Calculate the mean number of red roses sold.
2 Calculate the mean number of white roses sold.
3 What was the modal number of roses sold of each colour?
4 What was the range of the number of each colour of rose sold?
5 If you were managing a florist shop would you prefer to sell your flowers with a frequency distribution (selling pattern) like the red roses or the white roses? Explain your answer.

See page 31 for the answers.

Application of Number and Information Technology

Answers

p.17 Activity – Using percentages

1a £28.70   b £192.70
2   £40.04
3a £21   b £399
4   £53.08
5   1989 meals
6

Invoice No.			
Quantity	Description	Unit price £0.00	Total price £0.00
2	M1475 Reinforcements	3.49	6.98
4	M-1874	1.99	7.96
		Total cost	14.94
		Discount 10%	1.49
		Sub total	13.45
		Add VAT 17.5%	2.35
		Net payable	15.80

p.19 Daily takings

1 Saturday appears to be the most popular day (the tallest bar).

2 Thursday looks like half-day closing (the shortest bar).

p.19 Activity – Reading graphs

1 Wednesday is the least popular day (the shortest bar).

2 Saturday has the greatest takings (the longest bar).

3 Tuesday and Friday had the same takings (bars are the same length).

p.20 Activity – Using pictograms

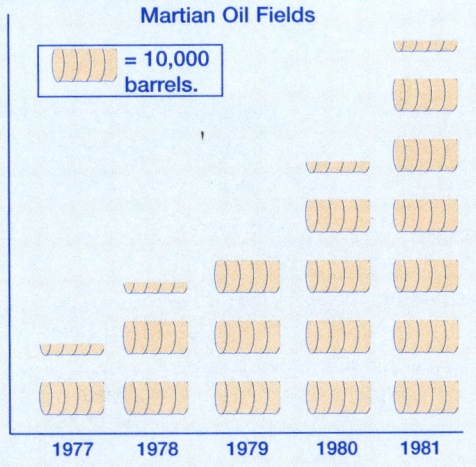

1 Martian Oil Fields

 = 10,000 barrels.

1977 1978 1979 1980 1981

2a 750–900   b 2150–2400   c 3000

p.22 Activity – Using measurements

1a 240 m^2 b 28 litres   c 21 litres
d 77 litres
e

	No of litres	Cost per litre	Cost per coat
1st Coat	21 litres	£1.20	£25.20
2nd Coat	28 litres	£1.20	£33.60
3rd Coat	28 litres	£1.20	£33.60
		Total cost	£92.40

2 The size of pitches can vary. The following assumes:

- the five-a-side football pitch uses all the sports hall, with two semi-circular ends one metre from each wall (diameter 13 metres), and a half-way line. All of these lines coincide with lines on the basketball court

- the basketball court is 26 metres by 14 metres (standard measurements)

- the badminton courts are 4.1 metres by 13.4 metres (standard measurements).

	No of metres	No of courts	Cost per metre	Cost per coat
5-a-side	Use lines from basketball		£0.05	£0.00
Basketball	200 metres	1	£0.05	£10.00
Badminton	100 metres	4	£0.05	£20.00
			Total cost	£30.00

p.25 Activity – Conversion graphs

1a 45 litres   b 5.5 gallons   c £19.01
d 7.5 gallons   e 375 miles
f   £19.01 ÷ 375 = £0.051 = 5p per mile

2a 8 square yards   b £71.82

p.30 Activity – Mean, mode and range

	Mean	Mode	Range
Red	5	3	11
White	5	5	2

You'd probably rather sell flowers with a selling pattern like white roses – evenly spread through the week.

31

Toolkit

Forms for you to fill in

In this section you will find a range of blank forms that you can photocopy and use to practise the skills you learn as you work through this book.

Application form

---

applicationFORM

the **Treasure Chest**

the enterprise Centre
Church Road
Brighton
East Sussex
BN15 0TT

tel 01273 764831
tel 01273 776644

Please complete this form in black ink or type.

Name ....

Address ....

....

....

Telephone Number ....

Date of Birth ....

Schools/colleges attended with dates

....

....

....

Examinations gained, please give dates and grades

....

....

....

....

Previous employers, dates of employment and job titles

....

....

....

....

Hobbies and Interests

....

....

....

**Referees.
Please give names and addresses of two referees**

Name ....

Address ....

....

Name ....

Address ....

....

Foundation GNVQ Business © Murphy and Palmer, 1995. Published by Thomas Nelson & Sons Ltd.

Forms for you to fill in

INVOICE

the Treasure Chest

To: ....
....
....
....

the enterprise Centre
Church Road
Brighton
East Sussex
BN15 0TT

tel 01273 764831
tel 01273 776644

Invoice number: ....

Invoice date: ....

Quantity	Description	Unit price	Total price
		Total cost	
		Less discount	
		Sub total	
		Plus VAT	
		Total due	

VAT Rate: ....

Cheque

Date _____ Rosetown Bank 38-05-06
STACTON BRANCH
3-4 WEST STREET, STACTON ST1 9RR   19

Pay _____ Pay _____

£

£   MS KHAN

00137 "000137" 38"0506: 37489216"

Foundation GNVQ Business © Murphy and Palmer, 1995. Published by Thomas Nelson & Sons Ltd.

Toolkit

Credit card sales voucher

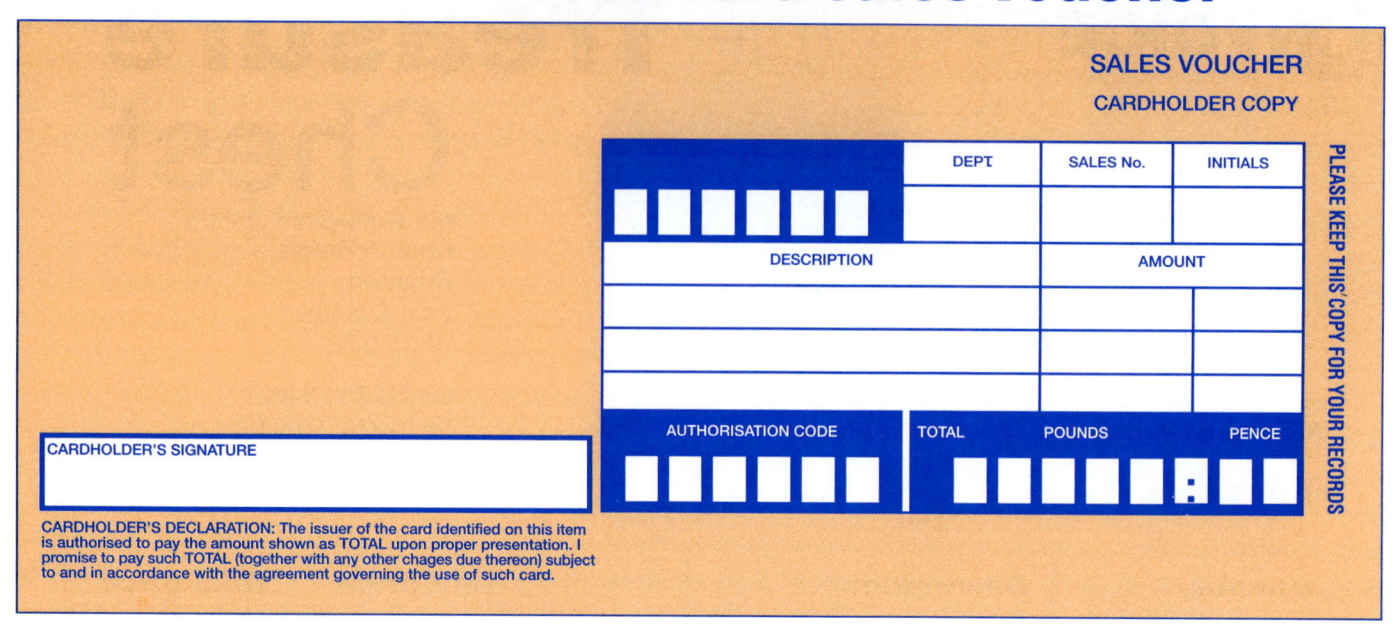

SALES VOUCHER
CARDHOLDER COPY

| DEPT | SALES No. | INITIALS |

DESCRIPTION | AMOUNT

AUTHORISATION CODE | TOTAL | POUNDS | PENCE

PLEASE KEEP THIS COPY FOR YOUR RECORDS

CARDHOLDER'S SIGNATURE

CARDHOLDER'S DECLARATION: The issuer of the card identified on this item is authorised to pay the amount shown as TOTAL upon proper presentation. I promise to pay such TOTAL (together with any other chages due thereon) subject to and in accordance with the agreement governing the use of such card.

Paying-in slip

Date _____ _____ 19 ___
Cashier's stamp

Rosetown Bank
STACTON BRANCH

38-05-06

Cash _____   MS KHAN
Cheques _____
       Paid in by _____
£   Number of cheques ☐

100659   "100659" 38⊪0506⦂37489216⊪"

bank giro credit

Notes £50
£20
£10
£5
Coins £1
Other coins
Total Cash
Cheques
£

Cash book

Debit (receipts)				CASH BOOK			Credit (payments)	
Date	Details	Cash	Bank	Date	Details		Cash	Bank

Foundation GNVQ Business © Murphy and Palmer, 1995. Published by Thomas Nelson & Sons Ltd.

Unit 1
Processing business payments

Introduction

Keeping track of the money coming into and going out of a business is the key to its success. This unit is an introduction to the different types of payments which are made in business. It will help you understand:

- different ways of processing payments
- how to produce and check payment documents
- how to maintain payment records.

Processing business payments

Explore ways of processing payments

This element will help you understand how businesses handle money and why it is important that they keep accurate records of payments.

By the end of this element you should:
- understand the different ways you can make payments to customers, suppliers and banks
- know all the different payment processing methods
- be able to use payment documents to process payments.

Why are payments made in business?

| Incoming payments | → | Business | → | Outgoing payments |
| Sales | | finance | | Stock, rent, lighting, heating, telephone bill, wages etc. |

Businesses make payments to purchase:
- **goods**, such as stock which will be sold to customers
- **services**, such as paying the rent on a shop, or paying the telephone bill.

These are known as **outgoing payments** as the business is paying out money.

Businesses receive payments from customers in return for goods or services; for example, a customer might go into a shop and buy a pair of shoes. Money which businesses receive in this way is known as **incoming payments**, as money is coming into the business.

For more about goods and services, see page 72.

Activity
Setting up a salon

Joe Blankson has inherited £20,000 from his elderly uncle who has recently died. Joe has just completed a hairdressing course at college and has been working part time in a hairdressing salon for the past two years.

Joe decides to open a hairdressing salon of his own with the money he has received from his uncle.

Before opening his business, Joe needs to have an idea of how business payments work. He knows he will have money coming in from customers who have their hair done and that he will need to pay general expenses.

This list shows Joe's expected payments and receipts in the first month. Make a copy, and tick either 'In' or 'Out' to show whether you think it is money coming into Joe's business, or money going out of the business.

	In	Out
15 wash and sets		
14 perms		
30 haircuts		
Rent for shop		
Business rates		
Electricity		
Telephone bill		
Bought shampoo/conditioner		
Advertising in local paper		
Leaflets delivered to nearby houses		
Wages for part-time assistant		

Explore ways of processing payments

Ways of making and processing payments

People make payments to businesses using a variety of methods, including:
- cash
- cheque
- debit card
- credit card
- electronic transfer of funds (including direct debit).

The type of payment they use depends on what they are buying and where they are buying it from.

Cash

People often use **cash** to pay for small items which are not expensive. If you go to a newsagent to buy a newspaper you will normally pay in cash.

Organisations use cash to purchase small items, such as magazines and flowers for the reception area, or tea and coffee for the staff. This type of cash is normally known as **petty cash**. It is kept in a locked cash box in the office.

Advantages
- Cash is quick and easy.
- There are no forms to be completed or signed.
- People avoid getting in debt when they pay by cash because they cannot buy items when they run out of money.

Disadvantages
- Large amounts of cash can be heavy and bulky to carry around.
- If cash is lost or stolen, it cannot be replaced.

What does it mean?
- Petty cash = cash businesses keep in the office to use for buying small items such as coffee and flowers.

Activity
How do you pay for goods?

Contact your local supermarket manager, and arrange a day when you may visit the supermarket and watch a checkout for a given time (for instance, 30 minutes). During that time, note how many people pay by the various methods available. Record this information.

When you return to school or college:
- work out the percentage of shoppers who paid by cash
- collect similar information from other people in your group
- key your data into a spreadsheet on the computer, and produce bar charts to show the proportion of shoppers paying by:
  - cash
  - cheque
  - credit card
  - debit card.

Which is the most common method of payment? Is this what you would have expected?

For help with using a spreadsheet, see the Toolkit on page 26.

Processing business payments

For a cheque you can photocopy and practise filling in, see the Toolkit on page 33.

Cheques

A **cheque** is another common way to pay for goods or services.

1. **Amount in words.** This is included so the bank can double-check the amount written in numbers (both should be the same). If there is a difference, the bank will not **honour** the cheque. The amount in words should be written from the far left of the cheque; after this any spare gaps should be filled with a line so no extra words can be added. Some people add the word 'only' after the amount for the same reason (for example, 'Ten pounds only').

2. **Sort code.** This code shows the bank and branch at which the account is held. The first two numbers of the code show the bank; the last four show the branch. This sort code, 38-05-06, means that Mrs Brown's account is with Rosetown Bank (code 38). Her branch has the code 05-06.

3. **Date.** A cheque should always be dated. If Mr Jay does not pay the cheque into his bank account within six months of this date it becomes a **stale cheque**. If you put a date in the future on a cheque, it is known as a **post-dated cheque** and can't be paid into a bank account until the date shown.

4. **Amount in numbers.** This should be written in the box, again starting from the far left. Any gaps should be filled in with a straight line.

5. **Name of the account holder.** The name of the person who wrote the cheque.

6. **Signature.** The cheque should be signed by the account holder.

7. **Account number.** This is Mrs Brown's account number. It tells the bank from which account to take the amount on the cheque.

8. **A crossed cheque** must be paid into a bank account; it cannot be exchanged for cash. Mr Jay will have to pay this cheque into his bank account. If the cheque did not have these lines on it, Mr Jay could take it to the bank branch written on it and exchange it for cash by **endorsing** it (signing it on the back).

9. **Cheque number.** All cheques are held in a cheque book and given a number. This helps people keep track of how much they have spent and see what has been paid on their **bank statement**.

10. **Counterfoil.** This part of the cheque remains in the cheque book after the cheque has been detached as a record of the cheque number, amount, date and the payee.

11. **Payee.** The person to whom the cheque is made payable.

What do they mean?

- **Honour** = when a bank pays a cheque, it is said to 'honour' it.
- **Bank statement** = a list of the money which has gone in and out of a bank account in a certain period of time

Advantages
- Can cover unexpected expenses.
- Avoids carrying large amounts of cash.
- Secure, as if it is lost it cannot be cashed.
- Counterfoils provide a record of payment.

Disadvantages
- Time-consuming to complete in shops.
- Sometimes restricted by the limit of the cheque guarantee card.
- Takes time for cheques to be processed and cleared.

Explore ways of processing payments

Activity
Writing cheques

Ms Khan is setting up a small health and fitness club, and is getting ready for the grand opening at the end of the month. In the meantime, she has had to pay some expenses. Photocopy blank cheques from the Toolkit (see page 33), and complete cheques for the following amounts:

- 1 March – one month's rent in advance, £700, payable to Harold Holdings PLC
- 3 March – business stationery bought from Paper Mates Stationers, £50
- 3 March – equipment (exercise mats, dumb-bells etc.) from Fitness Bits Ltd., £65.90
- 7 March – telephone installation charges. £35 payable to British Telecom

Cheque guarantee cards

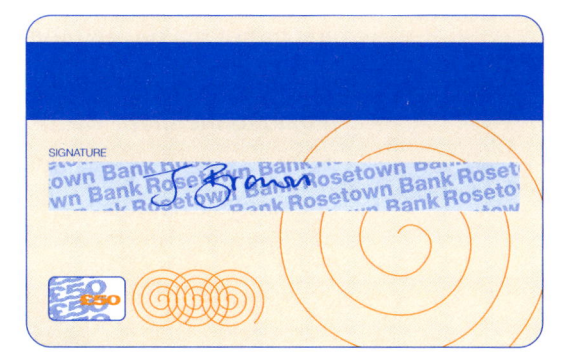

If you want to pay for goods or services by cheque in a shop, you need to present a **cheque guarantee card**. This shows your signature, account number and details of your bank.

A cheque guarantee card is proof that the bank will pay a cheque written up to the value shown on the card, even if you don't have enough money in your account to cover it. Most banks issue cards which guarantee payments up to either £50 or £100. Once your cheque guarantee card number has been written on the back of a cheque, you cannot stop its payment.

If you send a cheque in the post as payment, you don't have to send your cheque guarantee card as well. However, you may be asked to write the card number on the back of the cheque.

Accepting cheque guarantee cards

When you hand over your cheque guarantee card, the cashier checks that your signature and the bank details are the same as on the cheque. If you've spent over the limit on your cheque guarantee card, you will normally be asked to provide another form of identification, such as a driving licence.

There are two ways of processing cheque payments:

- **manually**. The customer writes the cheque and the cashier checks the details. The cashier compares the signature and account details to those on the cheque guarantee card, and writes the card details on the back of the cheque.
- **by computer**. Large organisations with electronic tills print cheques automatically.

What do you think shops do with the cash and cheques they take during the day? Are they left in the till overnight?

'Who do I make it out to?'

'We print cheques, sir.'

For more on processing cheques electronically, see page 43.

Processing business payments

What do they mean?

- **Voucher** = a document which shows payment.
- **Authorise** = confirm that you want payment to go out of your account.
- **Goodwill** = positive feelings about a particular shop, which make customers more likely to return.

Debit cards

A **debit card** is often called a **plastic cheque**, as like a cheque you can use it to pay for goods and services with money from your bank account. It is often combined with a **cheque guarantee card**.

When you pay by debit card, the cashier checks your account details and your signature, and produces a special **voucher** showing details of the amount spent and the date. After checking the details are correct, you sign the voucher to authorise payment. The money is then deducted (**debited**) from your bank account.

In some shops (especially supermarkets), you can also use a debit card to receive 'cash back'. You can ask for any amount up to £50. The cashier pays you out of the till, and the money is taken straight out of your bank account and repaid to the shop. The shop doesn't make any profit, but it does encourage customer **goodwill**.

Which is the debit symbol?

Activity

Advantages and disadvantages of debit cards

Copy and complete the following chart about the advantages and disadvantages of paying by debit card. Put a tick in the 'Advantage' column if you think something is an advantage. Put a tick in the 'Disadvantage' column if you think something is a disadvantage.

Write in some advantages and disadvantages of your own.

	Advantage	Disadvantage
It's a quick and easy way to pay		
It's easy to lose track of what you've spent		
It guarantees payment for the receiver		
You don't have to carry large amounts of cash		
Businesses receiving payment by direct debit pay a fee to the bank or card company		
If stolen, the card can be 'stopped', so the thief can't use it		

40

Explore ways of processing payments

Credit cards

Banks and building societies also issue **credit cards** – the best-known are Visa and Access. Credit cards enable you to buy goods or services on **credit**, and pay for them at a later date. You receive a statement each month, telling you how much you owe and giving you a date by which you must pay back some of the money. You are then charged **interest** on anything you don't pay back before this date. Some shops (like Burtons and Marks & Spencer) have their own **charge cards**, which work in the same way as credit cards.

If you have a credit card, you can buy goods or services anywhere which is linked to the scheme (for example, shops, restaurants and garages). Places that accept credit cards normally display a sign in their window.

Advantages
- If the credit card bill is paid before the date payment is due, no interest is charged.
- People with credit cards can meet unexpected expenses.
- Goods bought on some credit cards are insured against accidental damage.
- Credit cards can be used to make purchases in person, by post, or over the telephone.

Disadvantages
- Customers have to pay interest if they don't pay off the whole balance before the payment date. This can make the original purchase quite a lot more expensive.
- Businesses accepting payments by this method have to pay a fee to the credit card company.

What do they mean?
- **Interest** = a charge made for paying back money over a period of time. The interest you have to pay is a percentage of the amount you owe.
- **Manually** = by hand.

Why do you think some shops have their own charge cards instead of accepting credit cards?

Accepting credit cards

When you use a credit card to pay for goods, the cashier checks the expiry date and your signature on the card. Credit card payments can be processed in two ways:

- **manually**. The credit card and a sales voucher are run through an imprinter, which prints the details from the credit card onto the voucher. If the sale is for a large amount, the cashier telephones the credit card company to confirm the card is valid and to get an authorisation code to write on the sales voucher.
- **by computer**. Large organisations have an electronic link to the credit card company. The credit card details are scanned electronically, checks are made automatically, and the sales voucher is printed.

With both manual and electronic credit card payment, the buyer must sign the sales voucher to confirm the payment.

For more on processing credit card payments electronically, see page 43.

Processing business payments

Activity
Spend, spend, spend

Paula Mdebele has just received the new Visa card for which she applied. She is obviously very excited and decides to go out on a spending spree. She has been given a credit limit of £500, and the card does not run out (expire) for a year. During that day she makes the following purchases on her Visa card:

£20	Petrol
£36.99	Textbooks for her college course
£110	New coat purchased in Alders department store
£50	An exercise bike bought by telephone

1. Photocopy the credit card slip in the Toolkit (see page 34), and complete credit card slips for the transactions above.
2. How much did Paula spend in total on her shopping spree?
3. How much does she have left to spend before she exceeds her limit?
4. Paula also bought a magazine, a newspaper and a packet of mints from her local newsagent while she was out shopping. Why did she not use her credit card for these purchases?
5. Give one advantage and one disadvantage for Paula using her credit card to buy an item by telephone.

Electronic transfer of funds

Electronic transfer of funds saves having to carry lots of cash

Electronic transfer of funds is the transfer of money from one bank account to another by computer link. This takes place in one of three ways.

- By Electronic Funds Transfer at Point Of Sale (**EFTPOS**), when a customer uses a debit card to pay for goods. Money is automatically transferred from the customer's account to the shop's account.
- By using **credit transfer** to transfer funds from one place to another. For example, a large organisation which pays hundreds of employees can save time by transferring salaries to their accounts automatically. It lists all employees' account and payment details, and forwards the information to its bank. The bank is then responsible for sending the money to employees' accounts. Employees are given a pay-slip showing how much has been transferred. Credit transfer increases security, as organisations do not have to keep large amounts of cash in the building.
- By paying regular bills, such as rent, by **direct debit**. Money is electronically transferred from one account to another on a specified day of the month. This helps businesses to budget by spreading the cost of bills over the year.

What does it mean?

- Direct debit = an arrangement for payments to be made electronically from your account, usually once a month.

Explore ways of processing payments

Case study
Safeway supermarket

Safeway is part of the Argyll group of companies, one of the UK's largest food retailing business. Safeway stores sell up to 20,000 different products. A growing number of stores have specialist departments such as petrol stations, post offices, dry cleaners and coffee shops. Safeway employs over 66,000 people.

All 350+ Safeway stores use EPOS (Electronic Point of Sale) tills. This means that their goods do not need price labels. Instead, when customers go to the checkout with their shopping, the items are passed over a scanner. The scanner uses a laser to read the bar code which is printed on each item. The bar code is a row of numbers represented by lines or bars of different thickness. All scanners can recognise these codes.

As each item is scanned it is recorded by a printer, which produces a receipt for the customer. This lists each item purchased and the price charged, and is known as an itemised receipt.

A copy of this receipt is kept inside the till on a paper roll. This is known as the audit roll, and is used by the store to keep a record of payments received by customers, to keep a record of products sold, and to keep track of how many need to be re-ordered automatically by the system.

If goods are reduced in price, damaged, or their bar codes won't scan, the cashier can use a keyboard to enter the products' codes. Details of all items which are scanned or entered in to the computer through the keyboard are shown on a display above the till. The bill is then totalled.

Customers at Safeway stores can choose to pay using one of four methods.

- **Cash.** Cash is a quick and easy method of payment for the customer and the cashier. For this reason, some checkouts are reserved for customers who are paying by cash as they can be processed speedily.

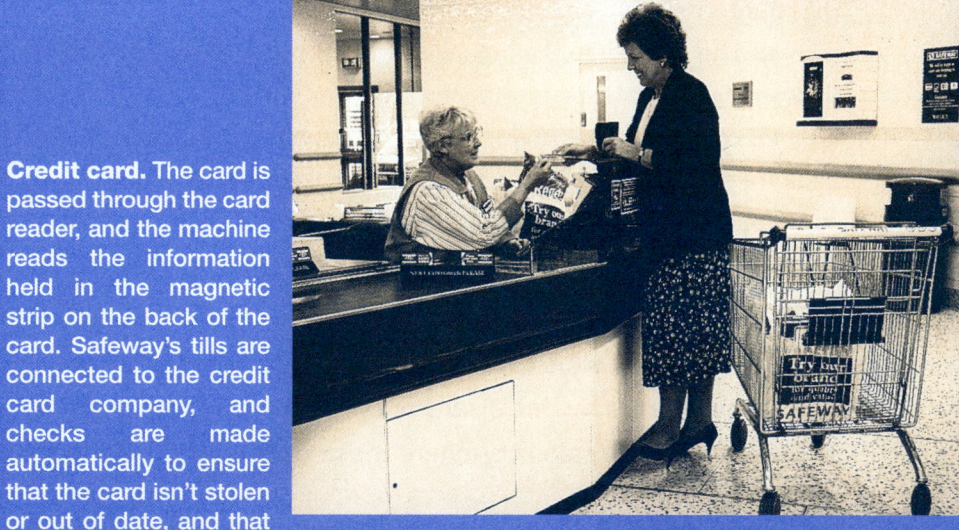

- **Credit card.** The card is passed through the card reader, and the machine reads the information held in the magnetic strip on the back of the card. Safeway's tills are connected to the credit card company, and checks are made automatically to ensure that the card isn't stolen or out of date, and that the customer is within his or her credit limit. The cashier then feeds a sales voucher into the machine, and the amount due, the date and the card details are printed. The customer checks and signs the sales voucher, and the cashier checks the signature against the card. Along with a till receipt, the cashier gives the customer the top copy of the voucher. The second copy is sent to the credit card company to claim the money due, while Safeway keeps the third as a record of the transaction.

- **Debit card.** The card is passed through a card reader which checks the card's expiry date, whether it has been reported stolen, and whether the customer is within his or her credit limit. A debit sales voucher is then printed showing the amount spent, the date, and the customer's name and account number. The customer checks the details are correct, and signs the voucher. The cashier checks the customer's signature against the card, and gives the customer part of the sales voucher as well as a till receipt.

- **Cheque.** The customer hands the cashier a blank cheque and a cheque guarantee card. The cashier puts the cheque into a printer attached to the till, which prints out the amount in words and figures and the date. The cashier then passes the cheque guarantee card through a card reader, and the computer reads the information held in a magnetic strip on the back of the card (such as the account number and expiry date). The system recognises if a card is out of date or stolen. The card details are then printed on the back of the cheque, and it is given to the customer to check. The customer signs the cheque, and the cashier checks the signature against the card before giving the customer a till receipt.

Processing business payments

Activity
Finding out about EPOS

With the agreement of your teacher, write to a major supermarket chain with a branch in your area. Ask if you can either make a visit to speak to the manager about the use of EPOS, or if someone can come into school or college to speak to the whole class on the subject.

Once the visit has been arranged, think of some questions to ask about EPOS. For instance:
- Do you use EPOS in your store?
- If not, why not? or Why did your company decide to use EPOS?
- What are the best things about EPOS for the store?
- What are the best things about EPOS for your customers?
- Are there any disadvantages to using EPOS?
- Do the checkout cashiers like EPOS? Why?

Think of at least three more questions to ask the manager during the visit. You will need to take a clipboard and some paper with you so that you can write the answers down (you may forget what has been said if you wait until you get back to school or college).

Once you have collected all your information, make a video for other stores, either telling them what a good idea EPOS is, or trying to persuade them not to use it (which you do will depend upon your findings). Your video should include as much information as possible. You may want to video the supermarket manager talking to you, if s/he does not mind.

For help with writing questionnaires, see the Toolkit on page 5.

For a paying-in slip you can photocopy and practise filling in, see the Toolkit on page 34.

Paying-in slips

Businesses paying cash and cheques into the bank must fill in a **paying-in slip** to show the amount of coins, notes and cheques they are depositing. This makes it easy for the bank cashier to check the amount received. The cashier stamps the paying-in slip and its counterfoil, and the business keeps the counterfoil – which shows how much was paid in and the date – as a receipt. This is proof to the manager or owner that the correct amount was deposited at the bank.

Small companies use paying-in slips to deposit their daily takings at the bank for safe keeping. Cash taken by larger companies, such as supermarkets, is collected by security firms like Securicor or Group 4. These companies protect the money from theft and deposit it in the organisation's bank account.

Paying-in slips don't have spaces for you to record payments by debit card or credit card. What do you think shops do with the sales vouchers they collect during the day?

Activity
Getting to the bank

Sandy works part time in a sweet shop. She has been trusted by her boss to count the day's takings and take the money to the bank.

The day's takings are:
1	£50 note
3	£20 notes
10	£10 notes
10	£5 notes
30	£1 coins
£10	in silver
£5	in bronze
cheques	for £19.99, £4.50, £5.80, £3.50, £20

Photocopy a blank paying-in slip from the Toolkit (see page 34). Complete a paying-in slip for Sandy to deposit the money at the bank. Explain why it is important for her to bring back a stamped counterfoil from the bank.

44

Explore ways of processing payments

Keeping payment records

Businesses need to do two things to keep accurate payment records:

- **collect information**. Businesses must keep payment documents as written proof of payments made and received
- **write down** details of all money received and paid out.

The purpose of payment documents

Invoices

An **invoice** is a bill sent from the seller to the customer. It lists the goods bought, and tells the customer how much he or she owes. An invoice must be neatly and accurately completed to avoid mistakes being made.

- **Purpose**: to give the customer a written record of the goods they have bought and how much they have spent. Invoices also prompt the customer to pay, showing when payment is due and how they can pay.

For more about invoices, see page 49.

Receipts

Customers are given a **receipt** so they know how much money they have spent, and where they have spent it. Receipts can come in a variety of forms; from a scrawled note on the back of an envelope, to a printed, itemised record.

- **Purpose**: to keep a written record of goods bought and to keep track of how money is being spent.

For more about receipts, see page 54.

Petty cash vouchers

When an employee uses money from the petty cash box, a **petty cash voucher** needs to be completed. The receipt for goods bought is attached to the voucher, which is then passed on to the supervisor or manager for authorisation. This is for security reasons – it means people can only use petty cash for business purposes.

- **Purpose**: to act as proof that money has been taken out of the cash box and as a record of what petty cash funds have been used for.

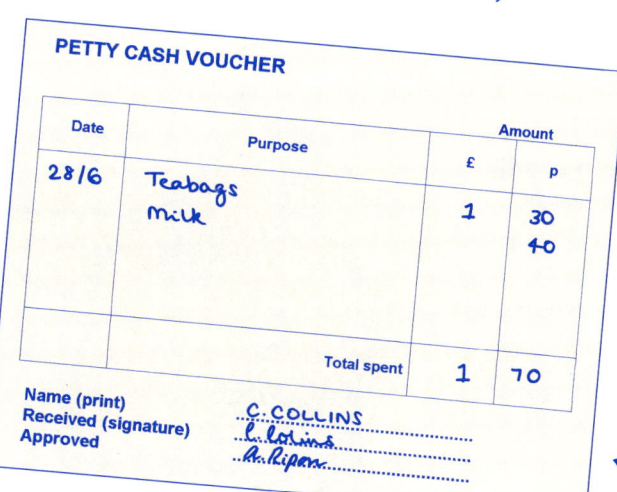

PETTY CASH VOUCHER

Date	Purpose	Amount £	p
28/6	Teabags	1	30
	Milk		40
	Total spent	**1**	**70**

Name (print): C. COLLINS
Received (signature): C. Collins
Approved: A. Ripon

For more on petty cash, see page 37.

45

Processing business payments

For more on paying-in slips, see page 44.

Paying-in slips

Paying-in slips are used to record money paid into a bank account.

- **Purpose**: to keep a record of how much, and when, money has been paid into the bank.

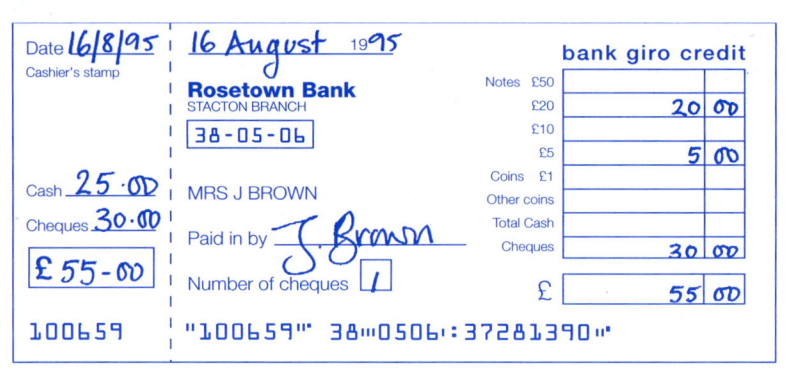

For more on cheques, see page 38.

Cheques

Cheques are documents which tell the bank to take money out of one account and pay it into another. Cheques going in and out of bank accounts are shown on bank statements.

- **Purpose**: to transfer money from one account to another.

Statements of accounts

A **statement of account** lists all the money going into and out of an account over a certain period of time (usually a month). A bank or credit card statement is a type of statement of account.

- **Purpose**: to provide a record of money going into and out of an account, and to show the current balance of an account.

Credit notes

A customer may be given a **credit note** if there is a mistake on an invoice (for example, if the customer has been over-charged or if goods are returned).

- **Purpose**: to take the place of a cash refund. It means that the goods will be replaced or an alternative of the same value will be supplied, depending on the customer's needs.

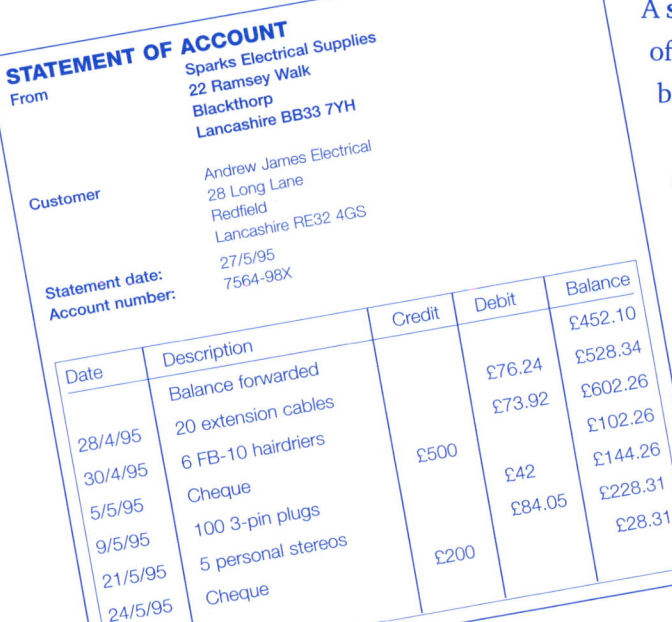

For more on credit notes, see page 54.

Explore ways of processing payments

Activity
Comparing receipts
Ask your family and friends to help you find examples of different types of receipt (for example, a supermarket receipt, a receipt for petrol from a garage, a credit card receipt).

- What do they have in common?
- What differences are there?

Write a list of information that should always appear on a receipt. Highlight three things which you consider are the most important. Why do you think these are so important?

Why is it important to keep accurate payment records?

It is important for a business to keep accurate payment records so that it knows how much money is coming into the business, and how much money is going out. Accurate records provide important information on:

- **current profit and loss** – businesses need to know whether they are doing well, and how much profit or loss they are making.
- **accounts** – businesses have to keep books to report on the amount of VAT (Value Added Tax) to be paid or claimed. Businesses employ accountants to check their accounts, and their job is easier if accurate records are kept.
- **cash flow** – cash flow is the amount of money going around the business. At any one time, money comes in from sales, and money goes out to buy goods or pay expenses. A business needs to know how much money it has available to spend on goods or pay in expenses, and how much it is receiving from sales.

For more about profit and loss, see page 79.

How much have I spent?

How much profit have I made?

Is my business doing well?

How much do customers owe me?

How much do I owe?

Processing business payments

Assignment
Wright's Corner Shop

Setting the scene
Your local corner shop is run by Mr and Mrs Wright. At the moment, they will only accept payment by cash. Their shop is losing customers and they think it may be because they won't take payment by cheque or card.

The Wrights know that you are doing a business studies course, and Mrs Wright has asked you to help her understand different ways of making payments. She also wants you to write out, simply, what she and Mr Wright could do to encourage customers to use different payment methods.

Task 1
Individually

Write a paragraph on why you think people tend to use one type of payment method rather than another. Refer to your own family and your friends, or to your own preferences.

Task 2
As a group

a Give examples of the most common ways that customers pay for goods/services.

b Describe the payment methods that the Wright's shop could use.

c Write a simple report for Mr Wright, explaining what happens when taking payments by cheque or card.

d Do you think Mr Wright should buy a new, computerised till? Advise him on this in your report, and explain why you give this advice.

Task 3
As a group

Carry out a survey of payment methods.

a Draw up an observation sheet you can use to collect data.

b Write or telephone the local store to ask permission for your group to visit and observe ways that customers pay for their purchases.

Task 4
Individually

a Design a poster or leaflet to show customers alternative ways of making payments. Include pictures, sketches, charts and so on, to make it bright and attractive.

b Copy and complete the table below.

Ways of making payments	Reason for payment	Document used	Manual or computer	Why is accuracy important?
Cash				
Cheque				
Debit card				
Credit card				

Task 5
As a group

a Arrange to visit the accounts department of the business to find out:
- differences in the ways incoming and outgoing payments are made
- the various methods of making payments
- payment processing methods used
- payment documents used
- why it is important to keep accurate payment records.

b Prepare a list of questions to ask on your visit.

c Write a report on your visit. You should cover:
- the ways the business pays for goods/services
- the payment processing methods used by the business (manual or computerised)
- the payment documents used and their purpose.

d Copy and complete the table below.

Ways of making payments	Reason for payment	Document used	Manual or computer	Why is accuracy important?
Cash				
Cheque				
Debit card				
Credit card				
Electronic funds transfer				
Paying-in slips				

Opportunities to collect evidence
In this assignment you should cover:

Element 1.1
- PC1
- PC2
- PC3
- PC4
- PC5

Communication
Element 1.2
Element 1.3

Information Technology
Element 1.2

Application of Number
Element 1.1

Produce and check payment documents

In this element we will look at how to produce and check payment documents. By the end of the element you should:
- be able to produce legible invoices for payment
- know how to check that calculations on invoices are correct and identify and correct any mistakes
- be able to demonstrate different methods of paying invoices
- be able to produce documents which prove payment has been made.

If invoices are unclear, mistakes are made

Producing invoices

An **invoice** is a bill sent from a seller to a customer who has purchased goods or services. It gives the customer a written record of the goods or services bought, where they were bought from, and how much they cost. It also tells the customer how soon the bill needs to be paid and what methods of payment can be used.

Invoices must be **legible** – clear and easy to read and understand. This is to avoid mistakes and misunderstandings.

Activity
Invoice totals

To fill in the total price on an invoice, you need to multiply the quantity by the unit price. Photocopy two invoices from the Toolkit (see page 33), fill in the information on the right, and then complete the total price in the final column.

See page 66 for the answers.

Quantity	Description	Unit price (£)	Total price (£)
10	Pillowcases	1.50	
20	Single sheets	7.50	
5	Bedspreads	35.00	
20	Double sheets	13.00	

Quantity	Description	Unit price (£)	Total price (£)
20	Bath towels	12.00	
15	Hand towels	7.00	
50	Flannels	0.99	

What's on an invoice?

An invoice usually shows:
- an invoice number
- the date the invoice was produced
- the customer's account number, if there is one
- a description of the goods or services bought
- the price per item
- the total price, including **VAT** and any **discounts**
- methods of payment accepted
- how soon payment is due.

For an invoice you can photocopy and practise filling in, see the Toolkit on page 33.

Processing business payments

Discounts

A **discount** is a sum of money which is taken off the normal cost price. A discount can be given to customers:
- for paying a bill quickly
- for paying by cash
- to encourage people to buy.

There are three main types of discount:
- cash discount – given for prompt payment
- trade discount – when businesses in the same industry reduce the price they charge each other for goods and services
- bulk purchase discount – when the more you buy, the cheaper each item becomes.

'Do you realise that as you're buying five you'll get a 10% discount?'

For more on discounts, see page 62.

Value added tax

Value added tax (VAT) is an amount of money added to the value of most of the goods or services we buy, worked out as a percentage of their total cost. The amount of VAT we pay is set by a government department, HM Customs and Excise, and changes from time to time. All businesses registered for VAT are given a registration number which they need to show on all their documents.

'I'm afraid the price shown doesn't include VAT'

Calculating VAT

VAT is added to the price of an item after any discount has been deducted. An invoice may show the final selling price of an item in a number of ways:
- the price excluding VAT (without VAT)
- the price including VAT (VAT already added)
- VAT shown separately, item-by-item
- the total VAT shown separately.

Do you know what percentage of the cost of goods or services is added as VAT at the moment?

Completing an invoice – some points to remember…
- write the customer's **name and address** neatly
- **quantity** – check you've put the right number of items
- **description** – check you've written a clear, short description of the item
- **cost** – check you've worked out the cost of each item (quantity multiplied by unit price)
- **discount** – check you've worked out the discount correctly, and written it in the right place on the invoice
- **total cost** – don't forget to add up the total cost and subtract (take away) the discount figure
- **VAT** – check you've worked out VAT correctly, and written it in the right place on the invoice
- **net payable** – add the total cost and the total VAT together

What does it mean?

- **Net payable** = the total amount to pay once discounts have been subtracted and VAT added.

Produce and check payment documents

Activity
Completing invoices
Photocopy three blank invoices from the Toolkit (see page 33), and make out invoices for the following.

Bells Buttons and Bows
95 Trade Street
London EC41 2GH

10m of taffeta at £1.75 per metre
40m of nylon taffeta at £4.50 per metre
35m of rayon brocade at £4.40 per metre
30m nylon chiffon at £3.00 per metre
VAT 17.5%, 10% trade discount

Webb Furniture
Unit 5
West One Trading Estate
London WH1 2BB

4 bookshelves at £40 each
5 wardrobes at £150 each
6 beds at £100 each
20 dining room chairs at £50 each
VAT 17.5%

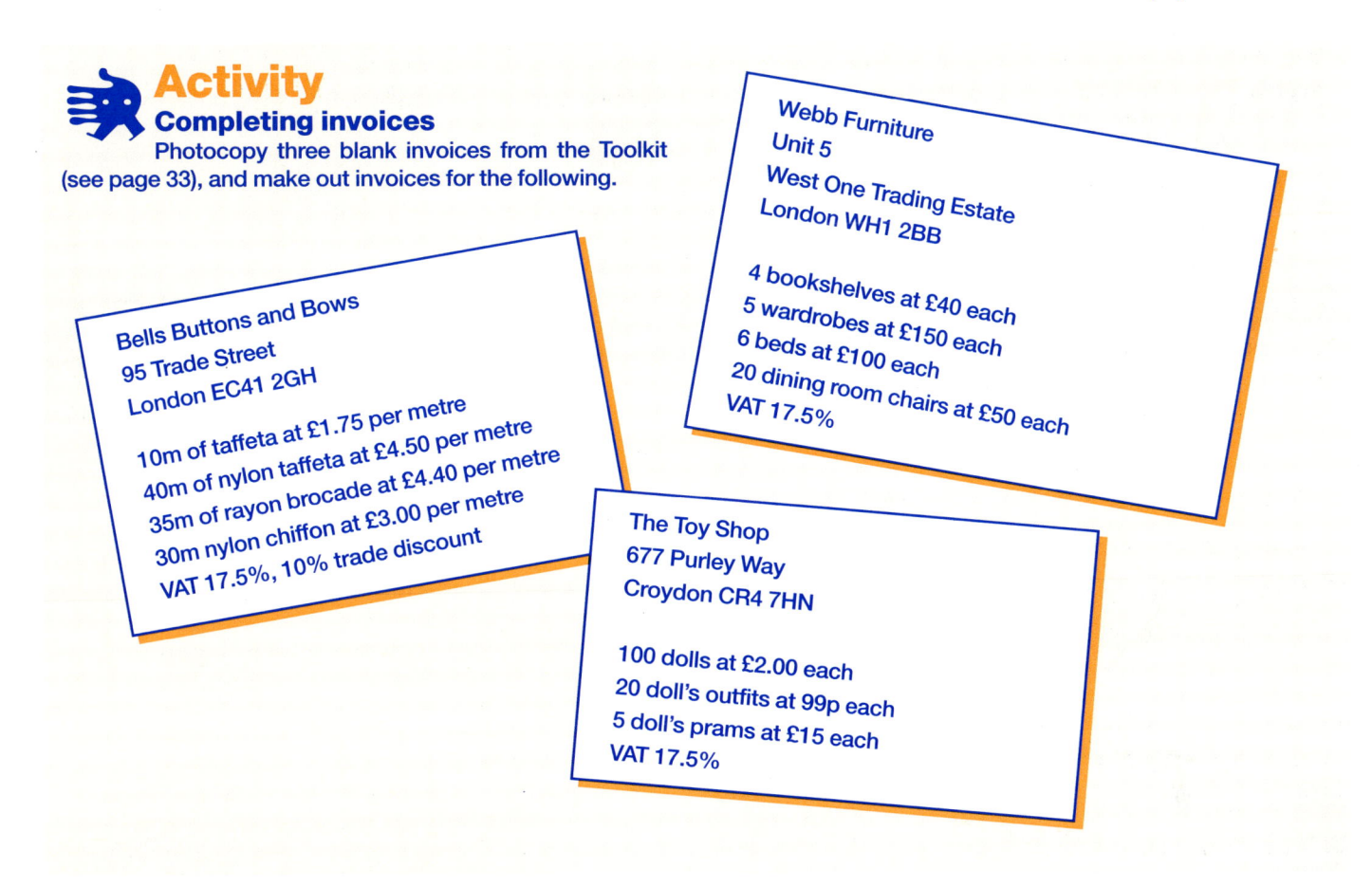

The Toy Shop
677 Purley Way
Croydon CR4 7HN

100 dolls at £2.00 each
20 doll's outfits at 99p each
5 doll's prams at £15 each
VAT 17.5%

Checking invoices

When a business receives invoices, it checks them carefully to make sure they're accurate before paying them.

DISCOUNT FURNITURE CENTRE
RAGLAN ROOMS
132 ASCOT DRIVE
CRANFORD SO9 5TY
Telephone: 01375 938746

Sold to: M. OLIVER
Invoice date: 27 June 1995
Address: 62 THE GLADES
CRANFORD
Post code: SO3 4DJ
Order no: 01395

Quantity and description	Unit price	
1 OSLO 3FT PINE BED	68.00	68.00
LESS 10% DISCOUNT FOR CASH		6.80
SUB TOTAL		61.20
PLUS VAT		10.71

VAT rate: 17.5%
TOTAL: £71.91
Order number: 363217

Description of items sold
Is this what you ordered?

Quantity
The number of goods sent – is this the amount you ordered?

VAT
Check the calculation is correct. If it says 17.5%, then this should be 17.5% of the total cost after discounts have been taken away.

Invoice number
Used as a reference number for payment and checking.

Unit price
The price per item. Is this the same as the amount quoted on the price list?

Discounts
This is a percentage reduction of the normal cost price. Check the amount shown is correct. A discount is taken away from the total price.

Total price
Multiply the quantity by the unit price. Is this figure correct?

51

Processing business payments

Activity
Spot the mistakes

The following invoices have been completed, based on the price list below. How many mistakes can you spot?

Order ref.	Description	Price per pack (£)
M-1435	A4 bank paper	2.49
M-1436	A4 typing bond	1.99
M-1437	A4 recycled paper	2.50
M-1345	A4 woven paper	2.99
M-1352	White envelopes	25.99
M-1417	'Fragile' labels	2.25
M-1687	Invisible labels	28.00 (per 800)
M-1517	500 address labels	5.50
M-1454	Reinforcement rings	0.50

STEVE'S STATIONERY
23 Bracken Place
Newtown
Liverpool L3 1DG

Invoice no

Quantity	Description	Unit price	Total cost
		£0.00	£0.00
2	A4 bank paper (M-1435)	3.49	6.98
1	Reinforcements (M-1454)	0.50	0.50
1	M-1436 typing bond	1.99	1.99
			0.00
			0.00
			0.00
	Total cost		9.47
	Discount 10%		0.95
	Sub total		8.52
	Add VAT 17.5%		1.49
	Net payable		10.01

STEVE'S STATIONERY
23 Bracken Place
Newtown
Liverpool L3 1DG

Invoice no

Quantity	Description	Unit price	Total cost
		£0.00	£0.00
		2.50	35.00
10	M-1437 A4 recycled paper	2.99	17.94
6	M-1345 A4 woven paper	26.99	53.98
2	M-1352 White envelopes	5.50	5.50
1	M-1517 Address labels	0.00	0.00
	Total cost		112.42
	Discount 10%		11.24
	Sub total		101.18
	Add VAT 17.5%		17.71
	Net payable		118.88

STEVE'S STATIONERY
23 Bracken Place
Newtown
Liverpool L3 1DG

Invoice no

Quantity	Description	Unit price	Total cost
20		£0.00	£0.00
10	M-1687 Labels	28.00	560.00
10	M-1517 Address labels	5.50	55.00
100	M-1417 Fragile labels	2.50	25.00
25	M-1454 Reinforcement rings	0.50	50.00
	M-1435 Typing bond	2.45	61.25
			0.00
	Total cost		751.25
	Discount 10%		75.13
	Sub total		676.13
	Add VAT 17.5%		67.61
	Net payable		743.74

52

Produce and check payment documents

Methods of paying invoices

Invoices can be paid in a number of ways.

Cash

When an invoice is paid by cash, the customer usually pays over the counter at a shop, the bank or a post office. Small bills are usually paid by cash.
- Payment by cash is a **manual** transaction, but
- cash payments can be registered on a **computerised** cash register, with the customer's receipts produced by the computer.

Cheque

A cheque can be used to pay bills in person (in a bank, shop, or post office) or by post. This is a quick and safe way to pay bills.
- Payment by cheque is **manual** when the cheque is hand-written.
- Payment by cheque is **computerised** if a shop prints the cheque.

Debit card

Customers can also settle bills using a debit card such as Switch or Delta. They can either pay in person (by going to a bank or shop), or they can write their debit card number on the payment form and post it.
- Payment by debit card is always **computerised.**

Credit card

Finally, customers can use their credit card to pay invoices. They can do this by entering their credit card number on the payment form; by quoting their credit card details over the phone; or by taking their credit card, along with the invoice, to a shop or bank.

For more about these methods of payment, see page 37.

Case study
Paying the phone bill

Jo's Beauty Salon has just received its British Telecom telephone bill (invoice). Jo can choose to pay the bill in a number of ways.
- By cash. Jo can choose to pay by cash at the bank, post office or British Telecom shop. The bill will be stamped as a receipt of payment. Jo cannot send a cash payment through the post.
- By cheque. Jo can write a cheque for the full amount due, and either send it by post, or pay in person at the bank, post office or British Telecom shop. If she pays in person, the bill will be stamped as a receipt.
- By budget account. This means making payments monthly by direct debit – a set amount would be taken from Jo's bank account every month. Telephone bills would be for information only – Jo's bank statement would confirm the payment had gone out of her account.
- By quarterly direct debit. Jo could arrange for the full amount to be deducted from her bank account every three months, when the bill is due for payment. Again, her bank statement would confirm payment had been made.

53

Processing business payments

Documents which prove payment has been made

Have **you** paid your bill? These documents all prove that you have paid for goods or services.

Receipts
A receipt can be hand-written, typed or produced on a computerised till. It is proof of purchase as it shows the date, time, amount spent and method of payment. Companies usually keep receipts in their records, to show how they have spent money.

Credit notes
When a refund is made, the customer usually receives a credit note or a written receipt.

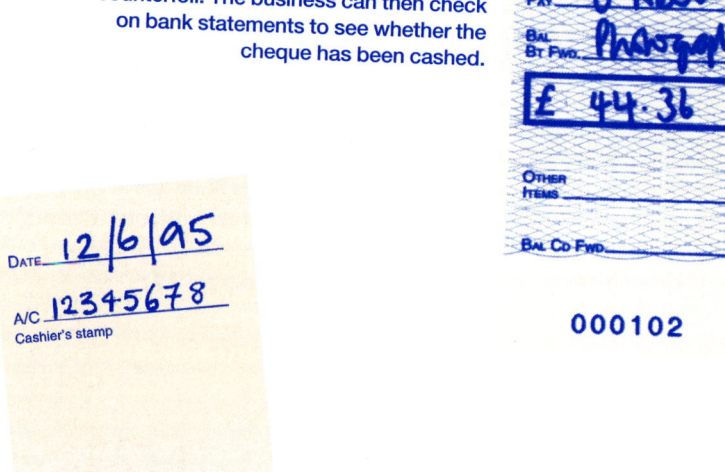

Cheque records
A business needs cheque records as proof of payment for goods and services. The person who writes the cheque is responsible for ensuring that a record is kept; for example, by filling in the counterfoil. The business can then check on bank statements to see whether the cheque has been cashed.

Till records
Businesses use till records to keep track of payments received and methods of payment. Some till records also show what has been sold during the day, which can help with stock control.

Paying-in slips
Like cheques, paying-in slips have counterfoils as proof that money has been paid in to the bank. The counterfoil shows the amount paid in cash and cheques, and is date-stamped and initialled by the bank cashier who receives the money.

Checking documents

It is important that all payment documents – including invoices and those which prove payment has been made – are carefully checked for accuracy. If you are paying a bill, you will want to check that the details are correct to make sure you don't pay too much; for example, if you're at the supermarket checkout you don't want to pay twice for your vegetables!

In the same way, businesses check payment documents carefully to make sure they are charging, and paying, the correct amounts. This includes checking:

- figures – are the calculations, amounts, quantities and totals correct?
- words and dates – can you read all the information clearly? are the details accurate?
- layout – is the document clear and easy to understand?

Produce and check payment documents

Assignment
Cristal's Health Club

Setting the scene
You are working as a receptionist at Cristal's Health Club. Your job includes the following responsibilities:
- producing clear, legible invoices for payment
- accepting payment for invoices from customers over the counter and by post
- producing receipts for money paid in
- checking calculations on invoices received and sent out, and identifying and correcting any mistakes.

Cristal's Health Club
Whether you're fighting the flab or trying to stay fit, Cristal's Health Club is for you. We have fitness programmes to suit all pockets and you will soon see the results when you start to visit!!

Join for a month and all you pay is the equivalent of £1 per day. Join for longer, and it works out even less.

What you get
- Comprehensive fitness evaluation (worth £10)
- Instant feedback after each work-out
- Individual supervision by trained consultants
- Unlimited use of all pool and water facilities

What you pay
One month's membership	£30
Three months' membership	£80
Six months' membership	£150
Twelve months' membership	£230

Other services available
Individual training session £10
(a supervised work-out)
Full fitness evaluation £10
(confidential evaluation, plus advice on diet and health)
Solaria sessions
£4.00 each
£36.00 for a course of 10

Task 1
Using a draw package on the computer, design a logo for Cristal's Health Club. Produce an invoice for Cristal's with its new logo. This invoice will be used to bill customers for services used. Remember to include all the usual features of an invoice.

Task 2
Look at the price list above, and complete invoices for:
- customer A for three months' membership
- customer B for one month's membership
- customer C for two solaria sessions and a full fitness evaluation
- customer D for a course of ten solaria sessions.

Check each of the invoices carefully, ready to give them to the customers. Initial each item as you check it.

Task 3
Write a brief description of how you would deal with each of the transactions if:
- customer A paid by credit card
- customer B paid by cheque
- customer C paid by cash
- customer D paid by debit card.

Task 4
Produce a receipt for the customers. Describe the type of receipt each will receive, and explain why.

Task 5
You receive two invoices from suppliers (right and below). Check the documents for accuracy, identifying any mistakes.

THE SPORTS CLOTHING COMPANY
21 Charnwood Gate, Carfield, Surrey, CA3 9DN
INVOICE NO. 13728   DATE 30.4.95
TO: Cristal's Health Club

Quantity	Description	Unit Price	Total
100	T shirts	1.00	100.00
25	Leotards	10.00	250.00
10	Aerobic shoes (various sizes)	15.00	150.00
		Sub total	500.00
		Less 10% trade discount	450.00
		Plus VAT at 17.5%	78.75
		Total	528.75

sports equipment company
99 PARK ROYAL TRADING ESTATE, LONDON NW10
invoice no. 9970   date 30.4.95
to CRISTAL'S HEALTH CLUB

Quantity	Description	Unit Price	Total
20	EXERCISE MATS	2.50	50.00
2	EXERCISE BENCHES	50.00	100.00
5	EXERCISE BIKES	20.00	20.00
2	STEP MACHINES	95.00	190.00
		Sub total	360.00
		Less 10% trade discount	36.00
		Sub total	324.00
		Plus VAT at 17.5%	56.00
		total	380.00

Opportunities to collect evidence
In this assignment you should cover:

Element 1.2
PC1
PC2
PC3
PC4
PC5

Application of Number
Element 1.2

Information Technology
Element 1.1
Element 1.3

Processing business payments

Maintain payment records

This element is about how businesses keep records of incoming and outgoing payments.

By the end of this element you should be able to:
- understand how to keep a record of payment over a time period
- check that payments are recorded on the correct date with the correct amount
- check that details of payments made are written clearly
- check that calculations made are accurate
- check totals using simple cross-checking procedures.

Keeping a record of payments

How often do you wonder where all your money has gone? If you earn money from a part-time job, you may well start the week with money and find by Thursday that you don't have any left. But can you remember what you spent it on?

If this happens to you, then you're not keeping track of your spending by keeping records. Keeping records just means writing down how much money you receive from wages or pocket money, what you spend, and what you spend it on.

Try keeping a diary of what you spend your money on for a week. It might be quite an eye opener!

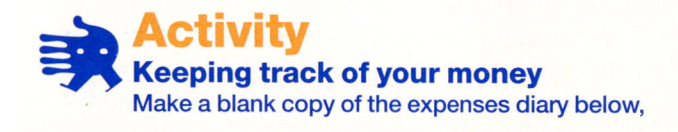

Where has all my money gone?

Activity
Keeping track of your money
Make a blank copy of the expenses diary below, and fill it in for a week to see where your money is going. Monday's expenses have been filled in here as an example.

	Monday	Tuesday	Wednesday	Thursday	Friday	Saturday	Sunday
Balance	£45	£15					
Spent	clothes £25						
New balance	£20						
Spent	magazines sweets £5						
New balance	£15						

56

Maintain payment records

How do businesses keep records?

Like you, businesses need to keep track of how much money they spend and how much is coming in.

The way a business keeps records of payments will depend on its size and how much money is available.

Manual or computerised?

Keeping records on a computer can save time and effort

Manual

A small business is likely to keep manual records. This means that records are hand-written in a book or on special paper called **ledger paper**.

Manual records:
- need to be written by hand
- mean you need a calculator for adding up and subtracting figures
- are fine if your business is small.

Computerised

Computerised records are usually kept on a **spreadsheet**. A spreadsheet allows you to enter and store information in a grid format on the computer. The format is the same as manual records on ledger paper in an accounts book.

The advantage of using a spreadsheet is that the computer can add, subtract, multiply or divide the rows or columns of numbers for you. You can make changes quickly and easily, and the computer will automatically calculate the totals again.

Computerised records:
- mean you don't have to work out the sums yourself
- save time by working out the new totals for you when money comes in or goes out
- are suitable for any size of business.

What records do businesses keep?

Businesses record payments coming in and going out in two main ways:
- on payments received sheets (manual)
- in cash books (manual or computerised).

What does it mean?

- **Ledger paper** = special paper with rows and columns where you can record details of payments.

For more on using a spreadsheet, see the Toolkit on page 26.

Processing business payments

Payments received sheets

These are a manual way for businesses to keep a record of all payments they receive.

Small businesses which don't have a till, and people selling goods at a market, often use payments received sheets. They are also used by businesses which receive payments through the post, such as mail-order companies.

Checking a payments received sheet

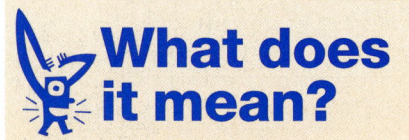

What does it mean?

- **Key figure** = the amount at the bottom right-hand corner of the cash book. The right-hand column and bottom row should add up to this amount.

Payments received sheet						
Date	Description	Received				
		Cash	Cheque	Credit card	Debit card	Total
1/8/95	Sales	£100			£20	£120
2/8/95	Sales		£60.50	£39.50		£100
Total		£100	£60.50	£39.50	£20	£220

By adding up the figures across the sheet, you can see the total payments received on a particular day (if it is completed on a daily basis). By adding up the figures down each column, you can see the total amount received by each method of payment.

Activity

Tally's tyres

Joe Tally runs a tyre repair shop in a busy high street. This is his payments received sheet for one week. Put these figures into a spreadsheet, entering a formula so that it calculates the totals for you.

1. What was the total amount Joe received each day?
2. What was the total amount received by each method of payment?
3. Do the totals in the columns and rows add up to the same?
4. Produce a graph to show how much money Joe received by different methods of payment (for example, how much in cash, in cheques and so on).

Payments received sheet						
Date	Description	Received				
		Cash	Cheque	Credit card	Debit card	Total
12/7/95	Sales	£150	£25	£10	—	
13/7/95	Sales	£300	£35	£30	£100	
14/7/95	Sales	£250	£100	£100	£20	
15/7/95	Sales	£100	£10	£45	£25	
16/7/95	Sales	£400	£30	£10	—	
17/7/95	Sales	£350	£100	£30	£50	

See page 66 for the answers.

Maintain payment records

Cash books

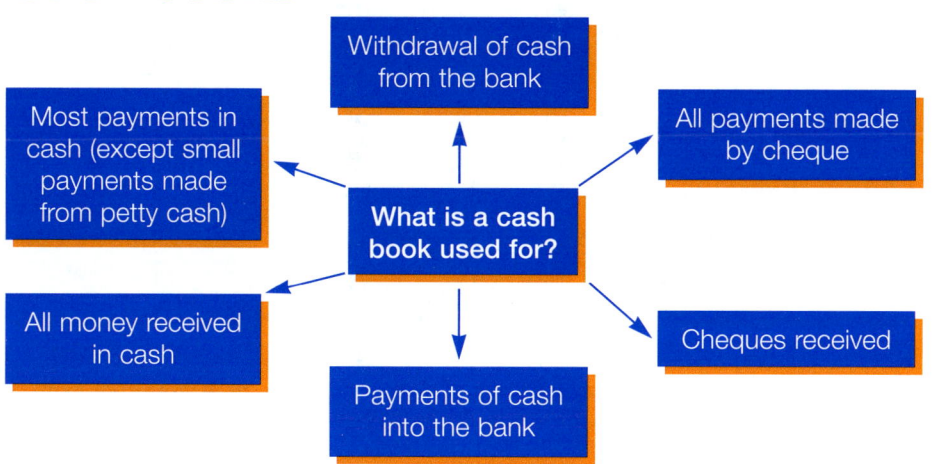

What is a cash book used for?
- Withdrawal of cash from the bank
- Most payments in cash (except small payments made from petty cash)
- All money received in cash
- Payments of cash into the bank
- All payments made by cheque
- Cheques received

What do they mean?

- **Transaction** = a payment into or out of a business.
- **Auditing** = examining a business' accounts in detail.

Cash books are a way of recording both payments received and payments made by a business.

It is important to remember that all **transactions** recorded in the cash book must be supported by documents such as receipts or cheque counterfoils, to help with **auditing**. For example, a cash or cheque payment can only be recorded in the cash book if there is a document showing the amount due, such as an invoice.

A cash book can be laid out in many ways to suit the requirements of a particular business. But the most common form is the **columnar cash book** (see right). Cash books can be completed manually (hand-written), or entered in a spreadsheet on the computer.

Paying money into the bank

How often businesses pay money into the bank depends on the amount of money they receive each day. If a business takes a large amount of cash, it may go to the bank daily; otherwise, it might make a weekly trip. For security reasons, it is not advisable to keep a large amount of cash in the business' cash box, as it may be stolen.

When paying money into the bank, two entries should be made in the cash book.

What is a columnar cash book?
- All receipts are shown on the left-hand side. This is known as the **debit side**.
- All payments are shown on the right-hand side. This is known as the **credit side**.
- Cash paid and received is recorded in the cash column.
- Cheques paid and received are shown in the bank column.
- The details column describes the type of transaction. It often includes a reference (for example, the cheque or receipt number).

Debit (receipts)			CASH BOOK		Credit (payments)		
Date	Details	Cash	Bank	Date	Details	Cash	Bank
			£100				£100

Write the amount being paid into the bank here. This shows your bank account has received money.

Write the same amount here, to show that money has been taken out of the cash box.

For a cash book page you can photocopy and practise filling in, see the Toolkit on page 34.

Processing business payments

Activity
Filling in a cash book

You should now be ready to complete your own cash book page.

Photocopy a cash book page from the Toolkit (see page 34), and enter the following transactions.

June 1	Paid £2,000 into bank
June 1	Paid rent by cheque, £250
June 2	Took £250 cash out of bank
June 2	Bought stationery for £50 cash
June 2	Bought materials for £175 cash
June 3	Received cheque, £300 from customer
June 3	Paid by cheque for leaflets, £125
June 4	Received £200 cash from customer
June 5	Paid £150 cash into the bank

To see what your cash book should look like, turn to page 66.

Withdrawing money from the bank

A business may want to **withdraw** cash from the bank (take cash out) to pay small bills. When this happens, again two entries must be made in the cash book.

Debit (receipts)				CASH BOOK		Credit (payments)	
Date	Details	Cash	Bank	Date	Details	Cash	Bank
		£50					£50

Write the amount you have taken from the bank here. This shows that the cash box has received money.

Write the same amount here, to show that money has been taken from your bank account.

Checking a cash book balances

At the end of the week, a business may need to know how much actual cash it has available and how much money it has in the bank. In order to discover this, it needs to balance the cash book. This **must** be done at least once a month.

To balance a cash book follow these three easy steps.

Step 1

Add up all the columns, putting the totals in pencil.

Debit (receipts)				CASH BOOK		Credit (payments)	
Date	Details	Cash	Bank	Date	Details	Cash	Bank
1.6.95	Capital		2,000	1.6.95	Rent		250
2.6.95	Bank	250		2.6.95	Cash		250
				2.6.95	Stationery	50	
				2.6.95	Materials	175	
3.6.95	Sales		300	3.6.95	Leaflets		125
4.6.95	Sales	200					
5.6.95	Cash		150	5.6.95	Bank	150	
		450	2450			375	625

Step 2

Work out the difference between the figures in the two cash columns, and the difference between the figures in the two bank columns. In this example, the differences are £75 for cash (£450 - £375 = £75) and £1825 for bank (£2450 - £625 = £1825). Enter these figures on the lowest side of the cash book, so both cash and bank columns total the same, as on the next page.

Maintain payment records

Debit (receipts)				CASH BOOK		Credit (payments)	
Date	Details	Cash	Bank	Date	Details	Cash	Bank
1.6.95	Capital		2,000	1.6.95	Rent		250
2.6.95	Bank	250		2.6.95	Cash		250
				2.6.95	Stationery	50	
				2.6.95	Materials	175	
3.6.95	Sales		300	3.6.95	Leaflets		125
4.6.95	Sales	200					
5.6.95	Cash		150	5.6.95	Bank	150	
		450	2450			375	625
				5.6.95	Balance c/d	75	1825

Step 3

The final step is to add up both sides of the cash book. The balances you enter are then shown as opening balances on the opposite side. Write balance b/d in the details column (meaning balance brought down). This is the amount with which the business will start the next day.

The cash book now looks like the one below. The two sides should balance. If they don't, then you need to see if you have made a mistake in your adding up, or if you have entered something incorrectly.

Debit (receipts)				CASH BOOK		Credit (payments)	
Date	Details	Cash	Bank	Date	Details	Cash	Bank
1.6.95	Capital		2,000	1.6.95	Rent		250
2.6.95	Bank	250		2.6.95	Cash		250
				2.6.95	Stationery	50	
				2.6.95	Materials	175	
3.6.95	Sales		300	3.6.96	Leaflets		125
4.6.95	Sales	200					
5.6.95	Cash		150	5.6.95	Bank	150	
		450	2450			375	625
				5.6.95	Balance c/d	75	2450
		450	2540			450	2450
6.6.95	Balance b/d	75	1825				

There should be £75 cash in the cash box. The business could check this simply by counting the money in the box.

There should be £1825 in the bank account. The business could check this by asking the bank for a statement.

The closing balances in the cash book were on the right-hand (credit) side, and were transferred to the left-hand (debit) side to see how much money the business had. If this had been the other way round, and the closing balances had been transferred to the right-hand side, it would mean that the business had no money in the bank and was overdrawn.

Activity
A cash book of your own

Over a week or month, try writing down a list of any money you receive and your expenses.

Enter the details in a cash book and balance it.

Do you think it is useful to keep a record like this? If so, why?

Processing business payments

Cash discounts

Businesses sometimes offer discounts if you pay promptly or in cash

For more on discounts, see page 50.

As we have already seen, businesses may receive or give cash discounts for prompt payment, bulk purchases or payment by cash. These need to be recorded in the cash book.

When a business receives an invoice for goods and takes up the offer of a discount, this is called a **discount received**.

When a business sends invoices to customers and offers a cash discount, this is called a **discount allowed**.

Activity
Working out discounts received
Work out the discounts received on the following amounts. The first one has been done for you.

Invoice total	5% discount received	Bank
£30.00	£1.50	£28.50
£150.00		
£78.00		
£25.50		
£62.90		

Activity
Working out discounts allowed
Work out the discounts allowed on the following items. The first one has been done for you.

Invoice total	5% discount allowed	Bank
£30.00	£1.50	£28.50
£56.99		
£65.00		
£74.00		
£23.40		

Case study
Cakes and buns

Brand's Cakes is a small bakery which supplies cakes to local firms. Being a small business, it often suffers cash-flow problems, and it needs its customers to pay on time so it has enough money to buy more stock (ingredients and so on). Because of this, it decides to offer a 10% discount to all customers who pay in full within seven days of receiving their bill (invoice).

When one of Brand's regular customers, Buns Bakers, receives an invoice from Brand's for £100, it decides to take advantage of this great offer. It immediately sends a cheque to Brand's Cakes for £90 (the total price of £100, minus 10% discount).

Buns Bakers then records this discount in its cash book. £90 is entered in the credit side as a cheque going out, and £10 is entered in the discount received column (on the credit side). The two amounts must total the same as the invoice (£100).

Buns Bakers' cash book

Debit (receipts)					CASH BOOK		Credit (payments)		
Date	Details	Discount	Cash	Bank	Date	Details	Discount	Cash	Bank
					8.6.95	Goods	10		90

When Brand's Cakes receives the cheque for £90 from Buns Bakers, it enters the figure in the debit (left-hand) side of its cash book. It also enters £10 in the discount allowed column on the left-hand side. The two columns added together should now equal the total of the invoice sent to Buns Bakers.

Brand's Cakes' cash book

Debit (receipts)					CASH BOOK		Credit (payments)		
Date	Details	Discount	Cash	Bank	Date	Details	Discount	Cash	Bank
11.6.95	Sales	10		90					

Maintain payment records

Case study
The GNVQ tuck shop

GNVQ Business students at Addington High School helped to plan and organise the annual Mufti Day event at school. On Mufti Day students can buy tickets for 50p and are then allowed to wear their own clothes for the day (rather than school uniform). The GNVQ students were responsible for designing, printing and selling tickets, and designing posters to advertise the event. As a reward for their efforts, it was decided that the group should share the profits from the day with the school.

The students received a total of £87.50. They decided to use the money to open a tuck shop at break and lunchtimes. The tuck shop would sell crisps, drinks and sweets bought from the local cash and carry.

The students talked to their teacher about what records they should keep of their business. They decided they needed to keep track of how much money they received each day from selling goods, and how much they had to pay for new goods at the cash and carry.

Payments received sheet

The students used a payments received sheet to record the amount of money they received each day. They couldn't afford to buy a cash register, as they needed all their money to buy goods for the tuck shop, but they did buy a cash box with a lock.

Each day a small amount of money was put in the cash box before the tuck shop opened. This was known as the float money. The students used this to give change to the first customers of the day.

After the tuck shop closed, all coins and notes were counted and listed on a payments received sheet. The amount received was the amount of money in the cash box minus the float money. This money was then put in money bags.

The student responsible for cashing up on a particular day signed the payments received sheet. This was important because if a mistake was found or there was a query they would know who was responsible for the cash at the time. At the end of the week, the money bags were taken to the bank and deposited in the GNVQ tuck shop account.

The payments received sheet the students used is a bit different from the one shown on page 58. This is because payments were only in cash. It was important, therefore, to show the breakdown of notes and coins received so they could be checked easily.

Notes/coins	Number in till	Amount received
£10	—	—
£5	—	—
£1	7	£7
50p	10	£5
20p	33	£6.60
10p	50	£5
5p	51	£2.55
2p	30	60p
1p	20	20p
Cash total		£26.95
Less float		£2
Total		£24.95
Signed		S. Lee

Spreadsheet

The students used a spreadsheet to keep an overall record of money coming in and going out of the business. The spreadsheet was set up like a two-column cash book, showing the date and details of money received on the left-hand side, and the date and details of money going out on the right-hand side.

The students entered a formula in the spreadsheet, so that the computer calculated totals and made adjustments whenever they added new figures.

Each day, the students entered the money they received from selling goods as a debit on the left-hand side of the spreadsheet. When they bought goods from the cash and carry, they entered the amount spent on the right-hand (credit) side. They made sure that they kept invoices from the cash and carry, filing them in date order. The balance figure at the end of the spreadsheet showed how much money the business had to date – the amount it had coming in, minus the money it paid out to buy goods.

Checking payments

Money in			Out		
Date	Details	Total	Details	Total	Balance
6.11.93	Mufti day	87.50	Stock	25.65	61.85
7.11.93					61.85
8.11.93	Sales	5.91			67.76
9.11.93	Sales	6.56			74.32
10.11.93	Sales	16.03	Stock	42.21	48.14
11.11.93	Sales	15.41			63.55
12.11.93	Sales	12.00			75.55

The students received a bank statement once a month, which they checked against the spreadsheet – the balance on the statement had to be the same as the balance on the spreadsheet. If it was, it showed that the students had kept an accurate record of money going in and out of the tuck shop.

Processing business payments

How can you tell if you are keeping accurate records?

- Your records of incoming and outgoing payments are neat and accurate.
- You use a payments received sheet, cash book or spreadsheet to record payments on a daily basis.
- You record payments on the correct date and with the correct amount to avoid confusion. This also allows you to check back if mistakes are made.
- You write all details of payments clearly.
- You check the accuracy of calculations using a calculator, or by entering a formula into a spreadsheet so that it calculates the balance and recalculates it when you make changes.
- You double-check totals by adding down the columns and across the rows. The total figure should be the same.

Assignment

The Strange Sports Shop

Setting the scene

Sid Strange opened a sports shop in Croydon on 1 November 1994. He had £1000 in cash, of which he put £900 into a bank account. He kept the remaining £100 in a cash box in the shop. For incoming payments he kept a payments received sheet, showing the date each payment was received and the method of payment. For outgoing payments he kept a copy of cheques written and receipts for cash payments in a box file.

After the first month, Sid had no idea how much money he had in the bank. To find out how much was in the cash box he had to keep adding up all the money. This was getting tiresome!

He decided to use a cash book to record details of money coming in to and going out of the business.

Can you help Sid set up payment records? Here is a list of tasks you should complete – use a planning sheet to decide which order to do them in.

Task 1
Using IT, design a payments received sheet. It should be clear and easy to understand.

Task 2
Write a short paragraph describing:
- the purpose of a payments received sheet
- the procedure for producing this sheet on a spreadsheet.

Task 3
Draw up a cash book, and enter the following incoming and outgoing payments in date order.

Money coming in, November
1   Sales made to J. Green, cheque £23.50
2   Sales made in cash, £34.00
7   Sales made to A. Thomas, cheque £45.00
13 Sales by cheque £45.00, by cash £78.50
18 Sales by cheque, £99.80, by cash £37.50
25 £200 paid in to the bank. £20 withdrawn and placed in cash box

Money going out, November
1   Paid rent in advance, £600.00 by cheque
2   Petrol for van, £20.00 cash
4   Payment by cheque to supplier, £150.00
15 Bought cash register, £200 by cheque
20 Paid British Telecom, £55.80 by cheque
23 Bought goods by cheque, £75.70
30 Paid window cleaner, cash £5.60

Task 4
Check:
- the payments are correct
- the dates are correct
- your calculations are correct
- your totals are correct.

Why do you need to do this?

Opportunities to collect evidence
In this assignment you should cover:

Element 1.3
PC1
PC2
PC3
PC4
PC5

Application of Number
Element 1.1

Information Technology
Element 1.3

Communication
Element 1.2

?Quiz

How much do you know about business payments?

Before you try the quiz itself, have a go at this word search to see how familiar you are with the vocabulary of business payments. Watch out! Some of the words go back to front and diagonally.

See page 134 for the answers.

```
P A I D C R E D I S R A
S P R E A D S H E E T S
E A C B S P S P C L Y D
S Y C I H T V O K A I I
A M F T B I R H A S C S
H E I M O D A T C C W C
C N O O O L I O O L T O
R T E N K D U H Y O D U
U S K L E N B O U G R N
P R T R T A L L O W E D
H J C S T P I E C E R K
```

Words to look for

credit	cash book	debit	purchases
spreadsheets	payments	record	sales
discounts	receipt	paid	allowed

1 You are shopping in a market for fruit and vegetables. You are most likely to pay for goods by:
 a credit card
 b cash
 c cheque
 d debit card

2 One main advantage of paying by cheque is:
 a it avoids long queues in shops
 b money is taken from your bank account the same day
 c it is a safe way of sending money by post
 d you can buy more goods

3 A post-dated cheque is:
 a dated in the future
 b dated in the past
 c sent in the post
 d illegal

4 The document used to pay money into the bank is known as a:
 a paying slip
 b withdrawal slip
 c pay slip
 d paying-in slip

5 The **main** purpose of an invoice is to show:
 a payment is required
 b payment has been received
 c the accepted method of payment
 d the balance of the account

6 The unit price on an invoice shows:
 a the number of items purchased
 b the price per item
 c the total value of goods bought
 d the price excluding discount

7 A discount is:
 a a percentage reduction off the normal cost price
 b added to the account of bad payers
 c the right of a regular customer
 d given separately to the customer in cash

8 VAT stands for:
 a value at transaction
 b vacant added tax
 c very additional tax
 d value added tax

9 The **main** purpose of a cash book is:
 a to keep a record of all money taken from a bank account
 b proof of purchase
 c to keep a record of money coming in and going out of the business
 d a statement of bank account

10 Money received in cash by a business is:
 a recorded as a debit in the cash book
 b recorded as a credit in the cash book
 c not recorded in the cash book, but placed in a cash tin
 d recorded on both sides of the cash book

Maintain payment records

Processing business payments

11 Payments received sheets are used for:
  a recording incoming payments
  b recording outgoing payments
  c keeping a record of bills paid
  d recording money paid out for staff wages

12 The main advantage of a spreadsheet is:
  a it keeps an accurate record of cash
  b it can perform calculations and alterations easily
  c it increases the use of information technology in business
  d it requires staff training

See page 134 for the answers.

Scoring

If you scored:
- between 1 and 5 – you're still not clear about business payments. Re-read this section, and then try answering the quiz again.
- between 6 and 9 – you have a reasonable understanding of business payments, but are still shaky on some points. Do you need extra information or practice in some areas?
- 10 or above – you have an excellent understanding of how businesses make and record payments. Congratulations!

Answers

p.49 Activity – invoice totals
- Pillowcases – £15
- Single sheets – £150
- Bedspreads – £175
- Double sheets – £260
- Bath towels – £240
- Hand towels – £105
- Flannels – £49.50

p.58 Activity – Tally's tyres

1.
   - Monday – £185
   - Tuesday – £465
   - Wednesday – £470
   - Thursday – £180
   - Friday – £440
   - Saturday – £530

2.
   - Cash – £1550
   - Cheque – £300
   - Credit card – £225
   - Debit card – £195

3. Yes

p.60 Activity – filling in a cash book

Debit (receipts)				CASH BOOK		Credit (payments)	
Date	Details	Cash	Bank	Date	Details	Cash	Bank
1.6.95	Capital		2,000	1.6.95	Rent		250
2.6.95	Bank	250		2.6.95	Cash		250
				2.6.95	Stationery	50	
				2.6.95	Materials	175	
3.6.95	Sales		300	3.6.95	Leaflets		125
4.6.95	Sales	200					
5.6.95	Cash		150	5.6.95	Bank	150	

Unit 2
Investigating business and customers

Introduction

This unit looks at how a business serves its customers and the factors which affect a business' profit. It will help you to:
- describe businesses and customers
- investigate costs and profit in business
- make a sales presentation to a customer.

Investigating business and customers

Describe businesses and customers

In this element we will look at why businesses exist, where they are found and what they provide. We will also find out how important customers are to businesses – after all, without customers, businesses wouldn't survive.

By the end of this element you should be able to:
- describe the purposes of business organisations
- identify and give examples of business organisations in a locality
- describe the main activity of different business organisations
- describe the services business organisations offer to their customers
- explain customers' expectations of business organisations.

Why do businesses exist and what do they do?

The scene: a typical kitchen on a Monday morning during term time
The time: 7.30 a.m.

hair cut by local hairdresser
cereal
bus pass from the Council
newspaper
hairspray
coffee
library book

You slump at the table, trying hard to wake up in time for a day's studying. You quickly eat some breakfast as you fix your hair and glance at the paper. If someone asked how involved you were with the world of business you might answer, 'Not at all!'. After all, you're a student, not a high-powered business person – not yet anyway.

However, you could not be more wrong. From the moment you wake up, wash, dress and begin the day, until you close your eyes at night, everything you do will have a connection with some form of business.

Everything you wear, eat, read, touch and take part in will be the result of one or more types of **business organisation**.

What do they mean?

- **Organisation** = a large or small group of people who work together for a shared purpose.
- **Business organisation** = a group of people who work together to make goods, provide services, or help people.

For more about goods and services, see page 72.

Activity
Businesses around us

If you look again at the breakfast scene above, you should be able to list quite a number of things which involve different types of business. For example, our student is eating a bowl of cereal produced by a leading food company, and her hair has been cut by a local hairdresser.

List all the other items in the scene which have anything at all to do with business. This will give you a good idea of how surrounded we are by the business world of buying, selling, making and using.

Describe businesses and customers

Desert island living

The only way you might avoid the world of business would be if you were stranded on a desert island.

However, if you managed to send a message in a bottle, the bottle would have been produced by a business, and the few clothes which protected you from the sun would have been manufactured by another business.

If you decided to make a shelter, you could be called a small building firm!

What products/types of business would you find it hard to do without on a desert island?

Businesses:
- are all around us
- affect every part of our lives
- do things for us
- make things
- sell things
- give people jobs
- make money
- make our lives run more smoothly
- hope to be successful.

What do the following organisations have in common?

British Telecom, Tesco plc, a public library, Oxfam, Lloyds Bank, The National Trust, J Smith & Sons (plumbers), RSPCA

See page 100 for the answer.

To complete your work for this element, you must investigate (find out about) the main **purposes** of businesses. Just by looking at the short list on the right you can see that there are as many purposes as there are businesses. A business' purpose depends on why it was set up and what it hopes to do. However, most businesses can be grouped into **one** of **three** main categories.

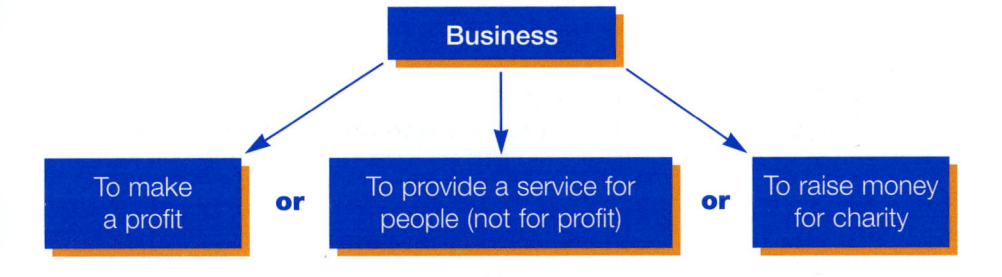

```
                    Business
                       |
        ┌──────────────┼──────────────┐
        ↓              ↓              ↓
  To make    or   To provide a    or   To raise money
  a profit        service for           for charity
                  people (not
                  for profit)
```

69

Investigating business and customers

'What's profit?'

'It's the money left over after a business has paid all its costs'

'What's to break even?'

'It's when you don't make a profit but you don't lose money'

'One that does good work for people in need'

'What's a worthwhile cause?'

Businesses for profit

You will know a business hopes to make a **profit** if it:
- is owned by private people, not the Government or the public
- has to make money in order to survive
- hopes to grow (expand) and develop
- tries hard to make its product successful
- needs to keep up with modern technology.

Whitbread Brewery is an example of a large business which hopes to make a profit. It employs many people, and provides many different services and goods for its customers – from pubs and off-licences to restaurants.

> Can you think of another example of a business that hopes to make a profit?

Businesses not for profit

You will know a business is **not for profit** if it:
- only has to break even in order to survive
- provides a social service for everyone
- tries to make people pay as little as possible for something
- hopes to help a group of people or the community, like a playgroup
- is one of the armed services (Army, Navy or Air Force).

The Post Office is an example of an organisation which hopes to provide a good service for its customers – wherever they may live, and however much it costs to collect and deliver their letters. It tries to keep its costs down.

> Can you think of another business which is not for profit?

Businesses for charity

You will know a business hopes to raise money for **charity** if it:
- aims to help others – at home or abroad
- gives money or goods to a worthwhile cause
- relies on donations from the public
- uses as many volunteer workers as possible to keep costs low.

Help The Aged is an organisation which hopes to raise money to help and give advice to elderly people. It holds fund-raising activities, such as flag-days, to help raise money. It also has shops which sell donated items. It is run mainly by volunteers.

> Can you think of another business which hopes to raise money for charity?

Activity
The purposes of businesses

Arrange the following organisations into three lists, depending whether you think they are for profit, not for profit, or for charity.

British Telecom, the National Health Service, Oxfam, the BBC, Sky TV, the Armed Forces, a local museum, the Fire Brigade, Barclays Bank, the Metropolitan Police Force, Debenhams plc, Age Concern, a donkey sanctuary, the National Art Gallery

profit	not for profit	charity

Describe businesses and customers

What's around the corner from you?

A walk in any shopping centre, **industrial estate** or **business park** in your **locality** will show you just how many types of businesses there are.

A closer look, or investigation, will also tell you whether or not these businesses only operate **locally**; are part of a much larger organisation operating **nationally;** or are **multinational**, operating worldwide.

Local businesses:
- are only found in one or two places
- are often small organisations
- employ a small number of people
- cater for local tastes.

National businesses:
- are found all over the country
- are well-known names
- are large companies with lots of workers
- have names, colours and logos which make them easy to recognise
- offer nearly the same services or products nationally.

Multinational businesses:
- are found in more than one country
- are **very** large companies
- often own many smaller companies worldwide
- produce and sell goods and services throughout the world.

What do they mean?

- **Locality = an area which is not too large and not too far away from where you live, work and relax.**
- **Industrial estate and business park = areas of land set aside for businesses.**

Which are national businesses? Which do you recognise? Which don't you recognise?

Investigating business and customers

Activity
Logos, signs and names
Look at this collection of logos, signs and names of different businesses. Try to decide which are national organisations and which are likely to be local. (Remember: you might recognise national ones.)

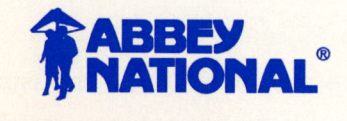

- ABBEY NATIONAL
- INTERFLORA FLOWERS WORLD WIDE
- C&A
- PETE'S PIZZA PARLOUR
- SURREY BUILDING SUPPLIES
- RAC
- MITSUBISHI MOTORS
- APEX CAR HIRE FOR EPSOM & EWELL
- OXFAM Working for a Fairer World
- THE PAMPER PARLOUR — BEAUTY • NAILS • TANNING

In a country the size of Britain there are a wide range of business organisations, some of which will be more familiar to you than others.

How many of the following would you have thought of?

- **Farmers** – growing crops, raising livestock, providing land for leisure activities (for example, golf courses).
- **Manufacturers** – using raw materials like steel and wood to make a variety of products (such as cars and furniture).
- **Retailers** – selling goods to customers. Retailers range from door-to-door salespeople to very large department stores like Harrods.
- **Wholesalers** – buying goods in large quantities to sell on in smaller quantities to smaller firms (also called **distributors**).
- **Transporters** – delivering goods by road, rail, sea or plane to wholesalers, retailers and so on.
- **Local authorities** – providing a wide range of services to members of their community (for example, education and health).
- **Construction** – building homes, offices, factories, roads and so on. Construction businesses range from small family firms to huge national companies.

For more on local authorities, see page 107.

Goods and services

You should now know that businesses:
- are varied
- are based locally, nationally or multinationally
- usually exist for **one** of three main purposes.

Now you can add one more piece of information to this list:
- businesses provide us with a variety of **goods** and **services**.

All of us, in modern life, use a large number of **goods** and **services**. Some of these are **necessities**; others are **luxuries**.

Describe businesses and customers

Activity
Goods and services you use

1. List all the services you and your family use regularly which you think are necessary.
2. List the goods you and your family buy regularly which you think are necessary.
3. List all the luxury goods and services you would buy and use if you were given £1000 unexpectedly.

Many types of businesses sell **goods**, for example:
- a bakery
- a chemist
- a newsagent
- a second-hand car dealer
- a timber yard...

Can you think of more?

There are also lots of businesses selling **services**, such as:
- a firm of solicitors
- an estate agent
- a window-cleaner
- a dentist
- a car-wash
- a leisure centre...

Can you think of more?

What do they mean?

- **Goods** = any items or products which are made to be sold. Think of them as things you can handle, see, smell and so on.

- **Services** = things businesses do for customers which customers do not or cannot do for themselves. Service businesses do the work for you.

- **Necessities** = things we need in order to survive.

- **Luxuries** = things we like or want but are not essential in our lives.

Activity
What do you know?
Which of these statements are true, and which are false?

1. If you worked as a volunteer for Oxfam you would receive a salary.
2. Marks & Spencer plc is a business which hopes to make a profit.
3. Profit is the money left after all costs have been met.
4. Collecting rubbish is a service provided by a local authority.
5. To break even means that a business owes a lot of money.
6. The Post Office is a business which aims to raise money for the community.
7. The Coca Cola company is an example of a multinational company.
8. Woolworth plc is an example of a business which is only found locally.
9. A local dry-cleaners provides people with a range of goods.
10. A road haulage company is a manufacturing organisation.
11. National businesses are often easy to recognise by their signs and logos.
12. A jeweller's shop sells luxury goods.
13. A business which does something for you provides a service.

See page 100 for the answers.

73

Investigating business and customers

The customer is always right

When organisations have to compete with each other for trade, it is very important that they treat their customers well. If customers feel satisfied with the service they are given, or the goods they buy, they will probably be impressed by the company and use it again.

Customer service

When a company decides that meeting its customers' needs is essential to the success of its business, it will try to ensure that:
- it creates a good impression
- every type of contact with the customer is satisfactory
- it is as near to being without fault as possible.

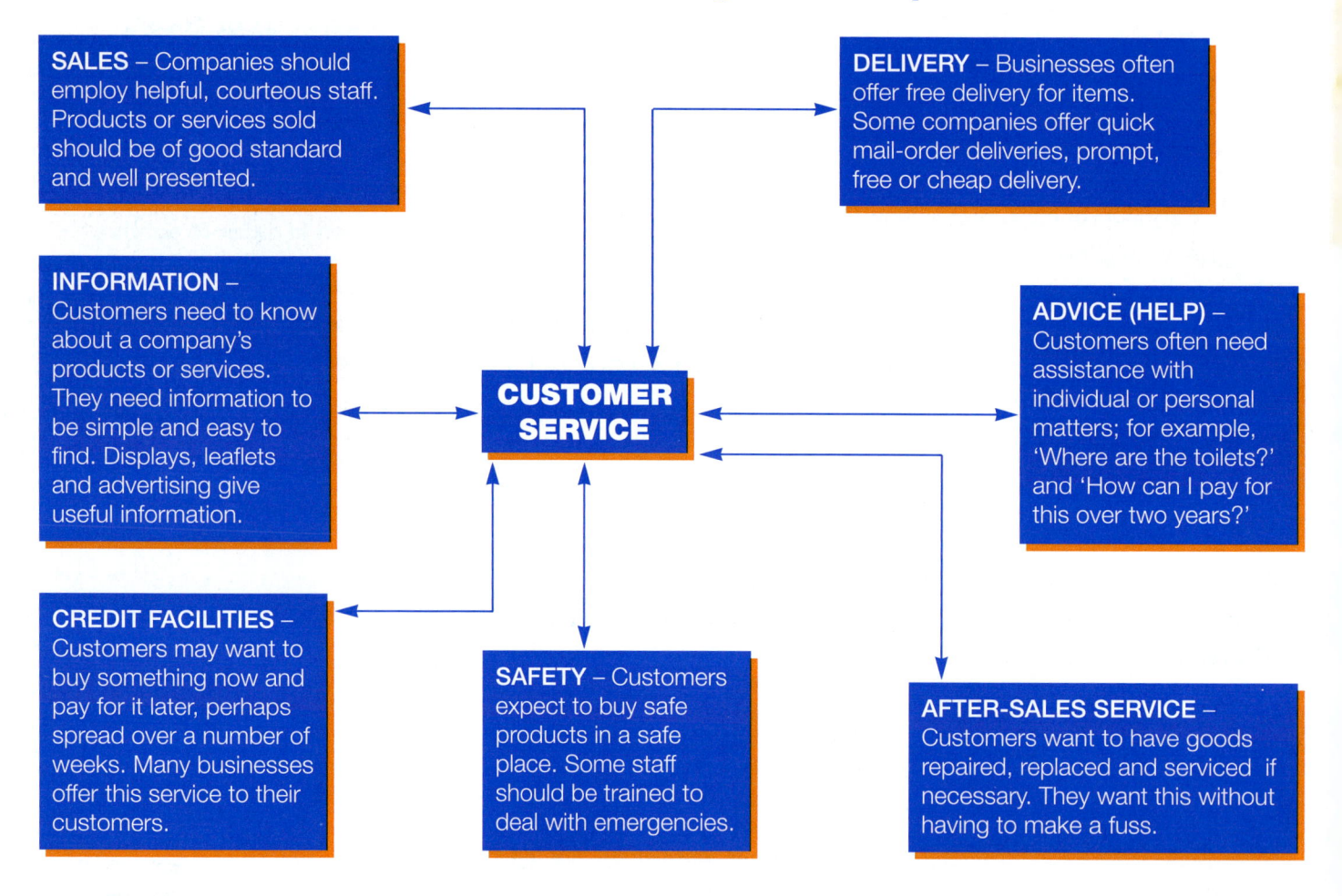

SALES – Companies should employ helpful, courteous staff. Products or services sold should be of good standard and well presented.

DELIVERY – Businesses often offer free delivery for items. Some companies offer quick mail-order deliveries, prompt, free or cheap delivery.

INFORMATION – Customers need to know about a company's products or services. They need information to be simple and easy to find. Displays, leaflets and advertising give useful information.

ADVICE (HELP) – Customers often need assistance with individual or personal matters; for example, 'Where are the toilets?' and 'How can I pay for this over two years?'

CUSTOMER SERVICE

CREDIT FACILITIES – Customers may want to buy something now and pay for it later, perhaps spread over a number of weeks. Many businesses offer this service to their customers.

SAFETY – Customers expect to buy safe products in a safe place. Some staff should be trained to deal with emergencies.

AFTER-SALES SERVICE – Customers want to have goods repaired, replaced and serviced if necessary. They want this without having to make a fuss.

For more on safety, see the Toolkit on page 7.

For more on after-sales service, see page 93.

Activity
Your own customer expectations

Over a period of a week, make notes about the times when you, or someone you were with, bought something as a customer. For example, you might have bought new clothes on Saturday, or a take-away meal.

For each example write about the following things.
- What impression did the business make – good or bad?
- Were the staff polite and helpful?
- Was any necessary or useful information clearly shown?
- Did the shop or office seem well cared for?

Report back to the rest of the group on your findings.

Describe businesses and customers

What aspect of customer service do these people need?

'I've had this CD player for two months and it's broken down'

'I've lost my mummy'

'I would like some leaflets about your range of fridge-freezers'

'I bought this toy for my son and a piece came off in his mouth'

'I'd like this bed, but have no way of getting it home'

'I'd like this pair of jeans in size 30. Do you have them?'

What customers expect of businesses

When someone goes to buy something, or is about to make use of a service, they have certain hopes about those goods or services. These hopes are called **customer expectations**. Customer expectations are not only to do with the actual goods or services, they are also to do with the quality of care and attention an organisation provides.

Usually, if customers' experiences with an organisation are satisfactory, most of their expectations are taken for granted. They are also more likely to use the organisation again, and/or recommend it to other people.

You can expect customers' expectations to be met if:

- they can buy the right product at the right time and find it in the right place
- they can pay for the product or service in a number of ways (for example, by cash, cheque, credit card, debit card)
- the products or services provided are not over-priced and are good value for money
- the product is packaged well (suitably for the product)
- service is polite and helpful
- the organisation, and its staff, are honest and trustworthy in their dealings (they do not sell shoddy goods or try to cheat you)
- the organisation is concerned for its customers' safety (both for its products/services and its premises).

For more on ways of paying, see page 37.

Investigating business and customers

Customer expectations satisfied – the CD player

- Visiting your local electrical superstore, you know exactly where to find the CD players as the different departments are clearly sign-posted and there's a store guide.
- The sales assistant tells you about the features and prices of the full range of players. They have all the models in stock.
- The assistant is very helpful. The instructions are explained and you are told about the different ways you can pay.
- At the counter the CD player is carefully put back in its packaging.
- At the till you read the notice which informs customers about refunds, exchanges and how to complain, if necessary.
- As you leave, you see large signs saying 'Fire Exit' and notice fire extinguishers. You also see a large board with instructions for dealing with emergencies.

Customer expectations not met – the gift hairdryer

- You want to buy your mother a new hairdryer for her birthday next week. Visiting your local 'discount' store, you cannot see any on display. You cannot find anyone to help you.
- There are lots of products stacked messily around the store. You trip over wires from a TV set.
- Tucked away in a corner you finally find a selection of hairdryers, but they aren't priced. There is still no-one to help.
- You decide to buy one, but are told that it isn't in stock.
- You settle for second best. You notice that the box is torn and battered, but are told that it is the only one.
- At the counter you are kept waiting while two assistants chat to each other, but ignore you.
- When you get it home you find the hairdryer doesn't work. Returning to the shop, you try to complain, but no-one is interested.

Activity
Meeting customer expectations
In your group talk about the following questions.
1. In what ways did the person who bought the CD player have his expectations met?
2. In what ways was the person who bought the hairdryer dissatisfied?
3. When have you had similar experiences when you've bought something (satisfactory or not)?

Ask your family and friends for examples of occasions when their customer expectations have or have not been met when dealing with different organisations. Write them down and report back to your group.

Describe businesses and customers

Assignment
Local business survey

Setting the scene
During the summer vacation you have been lucky enough to get a temporary job at your local Council offices. They are employing extra workers for a special project. You will be part of a team involved in conducting a survey of the different types of businesses and their activities in your local area. This information will help the Council make planning decisions about what types of shops and businesses it should encourage.

Your job is to collect the following information in preparation for the survey into businesses and the services they offer customers.

Task 1
Select three different business organisations in your area. You must choose an example of:
a   a profit-making business
b   a non-profit-making business
c   a charitable business.

Task 2
For each of the businesses, find out:
a   the purpose of the organisation
b   the type of goods it sells or services it provides
c   the type of customers it hopes to attract.

Task 3
Use maps to choose two or three streets which have examples of different types of local and national businesses. Show this area on a map or scale drawing, with a key to explain it. After visiting the area, record your findings by either:
- showing on your map or drawing where the businesses are located and whether they are local or national (use different codes and colours to do this), or
- completing a chart similar to the one below.

Types of local/national businesses found in each street

Name/type of business	Goods/services	Local/national
LES SMITH Car accessories	Range of goods	Part of a local chain
HAIR BY MONIQUE Hairdressers	Service	Small local business

Task 4
Prepare bar or pie charts to show:
a   the proportion of businesses which are local or national
b   the proportion of businesses which sell goods or services
c   the different purposes of the businesses.

Task 5
Select two businesses, one selling goods and one selling services. Arrange to visit these businesses to find out what sort of customer services they offer. Collect any leaflets they produce. Write an account of your findings.

Task 6
Select two organisations. For each business imagine you are a customer buying goods or using services.
a   What are your customer expectations of each business? (Look at the range for Element 2.1 PC5 to see what to cover.)
b   Interview some of the customers you see using these businesses. Find out what they think are the most important aspects of customer expectations.

Write an account of your findings.

Task 7
Use all the information you obtained from Tasks 1-6 to prepare a summary of your findings using your charts, maps, interviews, leaflets, and so on. Video or photograph any display to use for evidence.

Opportunities to collect evidence
In this assignment you should cover:
Element 2.1
   PC1
   PC2
   PC3
   PC4
   PC5
Application of Number
   Element 1.1
   Element 1.2
Communication
   Element 1.1
   Element 1.2
   Element 1.3
   Element 1.4
Information Technology (if work is word processed)
   Element 1.1
   Element 1.2
   Element 1.3

Investigating business and customers

❓ Quiz

How much do you know about businesses and their customers?

See page 134 for the answers.

1. The **main** purpose of a supermarket is to:
   a. serve customers
   b. make a profit
   c. deliver goods
   d. pay taxes

2. Which **one** of the following is there to make money for a good cause:
   a. a dentist
   b. a charity shop
   c. a library
   d. a bank

3. The **main** activity of an estate agency is to:
   a. sell goods
   b. give help and advice
   c. offer a service
   d. deliver goods

4. The **main** activity of a health food shop is to:
   a. keep customers happy
   b. give after-sales service
   c. sell goods
   d. provide services

5. Which **one** of the following is the **most** important service offered by a travel agency:
   a. delivery
   b. safety
   c. sales to customers
   d. after-sales service

6. A business repairs washing-machines free of charge while they are under guarantee. Which **one** of the following services has it provided:
   a. safety
   b. delivery
   c. information
   d. after-sales service

7. A local dairy provides its customers with fresh milk on their doorsteps. The **most** important service it has provided is:
   a. information
   b. delivery
   c. safety
   d. advice

8. The **most** important thing to a customer who is unsure which computer would be most suitable is:
   a. information
   b. safety
   c. sales
   d. delivery

9. Customers expect businesses with which they are dealing to:
   a. tell them how much rent they pay
   b. be honest with them about prices and services
   c. provide car parking space
   d. charge for information

10. Which **one** of the following would a customer buying an electric drill **most** expect an electrical store to provide:
    a. free home delivery
    b. an extended five-year guarantee
    c. a product which meets all safety standards
    d. attractive packaging

11. A multinational organisation is one which is found in:
    a. more than one town
    b. only one locality
    c. more than one country
    d. only one town

12. The Post Office is an example of:
    a. a local organisation
    b. a national organisation
    c. a multinational organisation
    d. a charity

Scoring

If you scored:
- between 1 and 4 – you need to know more about the different purposes of businesses and their activities.
- between 5 and 8 – you have a reasonable understanding of the main points covered in this element.
- 9 and above – your knowledge of businesses, their purposes and activities is very good.

Investigate costs and profit in business

We have already looked at the purposes of business organisations, and found out that making a **profit** is the aim of one kind of organisation. Now we will take a closer look at this type of business.

By the end of this element you should be able to:
- identify factors which contribute to an increase or decrease in business profit
- identify categories of business costs
- explain ways in which employees can contribute to business profit
- explain how employees can benefit from business profit.

You will also have a better idea of the costs a business has to meet, why some businesses do well and some don't, and the part employees can play in the success of a business.

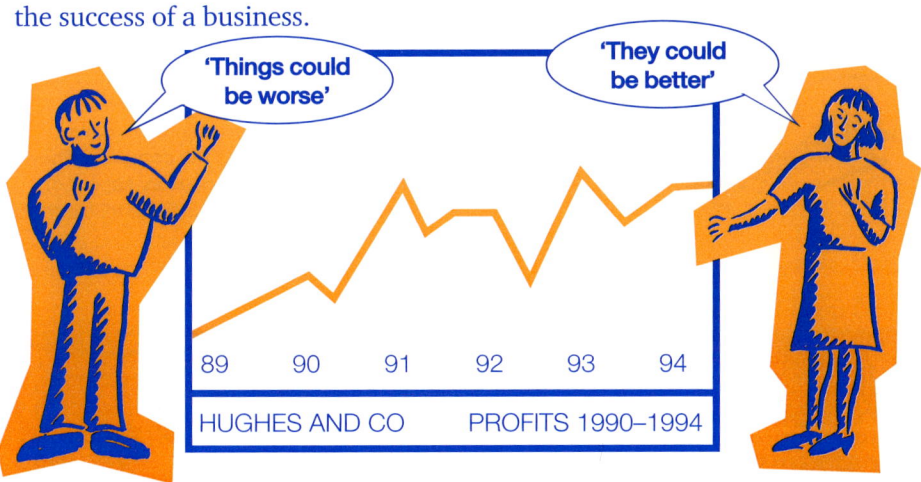

'Things could be worse'

'They could be better'

HUGHES AND CO   PROFITS 1990–1994

Most businesses which produce goods or provide services do so to make a **profit**. They would say that the more profit they make, the more successful they are.
- If a business' income (revenue) gets smaller or its costs (expenditure) get greater, profit **decreases**.
- If a business' income (revenue) gets larger or its costs (expenditure) get smaller, profit **increases**.

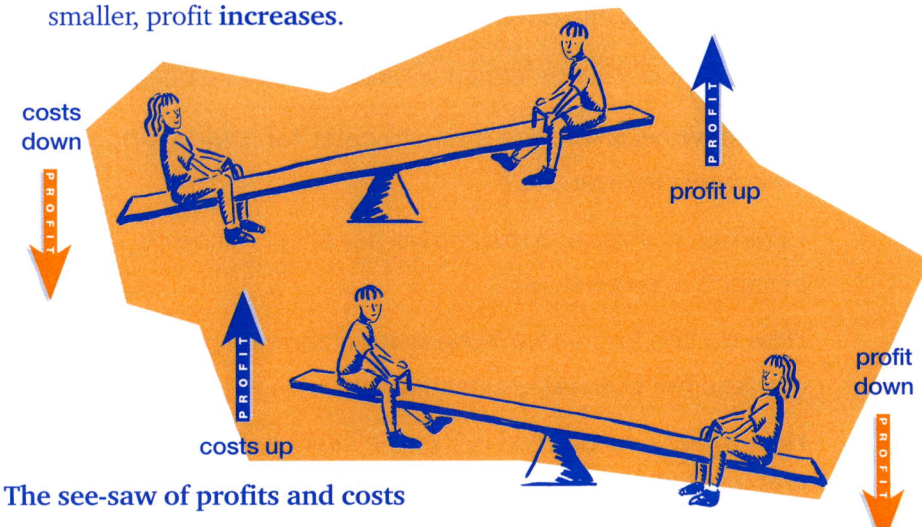

costs down — profit up

costs up — profit down

The see-saw of profits and costs

What do they mean?

- **Profit** = the amount of money a business has left when it has paid all its costs. In other words, it is what's left when its business costs are taken away from its income.
- **Business costs** = all the costs of running a business.
- **Income** = money received from selling goods or services.
- **Employee** = a person who works for a wage or salary. A worker, not an owner.

Investigating business and customers

Factors which affect profit

For more on sole traders and public limited companies, see pages 103 and 106.

Whether you are the managing director of a large public limited company or a sole trader who owns a fish and chip shop, the same basic factors will affect the amount of profit you make.

Customer preference
This is how people choose to spend their money. People in business must keep up with changes in customer preference. Age, amount of money to spend, lifestyle, gender – all affect customer preference.

Competition
How other businesses provide the same service or produce similar goods will affect the price a business can charge for its services or goods. In turn, this will affect profit.

Business costs
These are the various costs of running a business; from paying for the building and materials, to paying the phone bill.

Profit

Productivity
Productivity is the efficiency with which people in a business do their jobs. The more productive people are, the more they produce for a particular cost. A factory worker who can assemble fifteen televisions in an hour is more productive than the person who can only assemble ten televisions in the same time.

Management of business
The skill owners and managers have in planning and running the company. They must be able to control every aspect of running a business if it is to be efficient and successful.

Case study

Yvonne's flower shop

Yvonne had worked in a florist's since leaving school at sixteen, and had gained her NVQ levels I and II in Floristry. She had always wanted to work for herself, and attended a course run by the local small business association which told her a lot about being self-employed.

Not long ago, Yvonne saw a small lock-up shop to let in her local shopping centre. It was far enough away from her present job for the owner not to complain, and she would be the only flower shop in the centre.

She decided to sell a range of dried flowers and pot plants as well as cut flowers, as she knew both of these were popular with customers.

In order to raise the money necessary to open her shop, Yvonne prepared a business plan which she took to her local bank manager. She advertised for an assistant to work with her, someone who would like to train as a florist and was prepared to do a variety of jobs. She hoped to open six days a week to get as much business as possible. She also had a telephone installed so that she could take phone orders.

- In what ways is Yvonne trying to cater for a wide range of customer preferences?

- How has she tried to make sure her shop will be as productive as possible?

- How do you know that Yvonne has taken steps to try to manage her business successfully?

- How much competition is Yvonne likely to have from other florist shops?

Investigate costs and profit in business

What would happen to Yvonne's profits if...

PROFIT ↑

- she paid off her bank loan before she expected to
- the cost of flowers fell because of 'price-wars' between wholesalers – so were cheaper for her to buy
- she didn't need to advertise her shop any more, as she was well known
- she took her business to a cheaper phone company

- her van broke down and needed expensive repairs
- the cost of electricity went up
- she employed another member of staff
- another florist opened near her
- she bought new cold storage equipment for the flowers

PROFIT ↓

Activity
Factors affecting profit

1. How do you like to spend your money? Write a short account of your tastes in music, clothes and food.
2. Ask someone older than you what their tastes are in music, clothes and food. Write them down. Compare your tastes with the older person's. What are the main differences? Are there any similarities? If so, what?
3. Visit your local shopping centre. Identify which shops sell goods or provide services in competition with each other. Make a note of the following, and show:
   - where each shop is situated (show this on a map)
   - the type of shops in competition with each other (show these on a chart)
   - the type of goods sold or services provided (show these on a chart)
   - the steps each shop takes to attract customers (show these on a chart).

Categories of business costs

Business costs are how much it costs a business to produce goods or provide services. In order to survive, a business must make enough money to meet all the costs of running the business. As we have already seen, business costs are one of the factors which can lead to an increase or decrease in profit.

If a company has a sudden or drastic increase in business costs, a decrease in profit will normally follow. If costs get too great, the company may make a **loss** and face financial difficulty.

So, it's important a company is aware of the different costs it has to meet, and has ways of coping with them. The chart below shows the main categories of business costs.

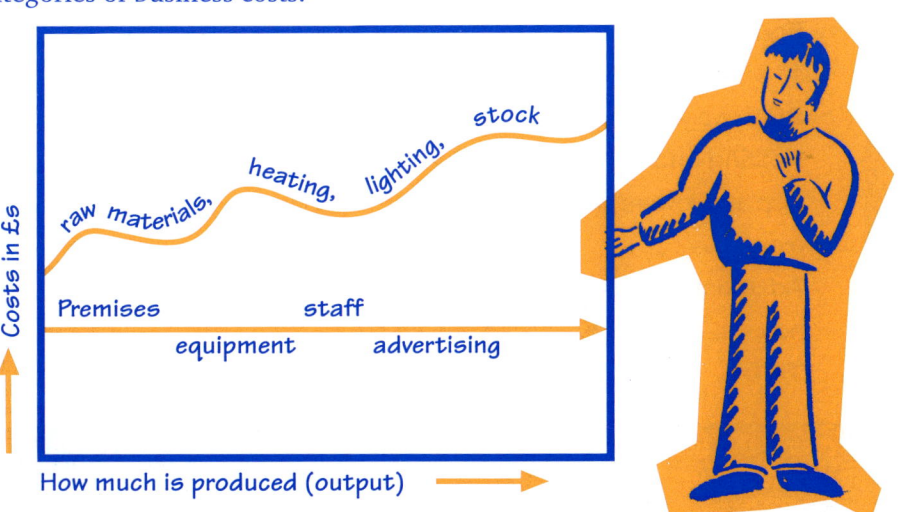

What does it mean?
- **Loss** = a company makes a loss when its business costs are more than its income.

Chart: Costs in £s vs. How much is produced (output), showing raw materials, heating, lighting, stock, Premises, equipment, staff, advertising.

Investigating business and customers

Costs which stay the same

If you look at the chart you will see that certain costs appear on the lower, flat line. These costs are:

- **premises**
- **equipment** (major items)
- **staff**
- **advertising**.

These costs are called **fixed costs** because they remain the same, no matter how many goods are produced. For example, the rent or mortgage on a shirt factory is the same whether that factory produces 2000 or 5000 shirts a week.

Costs which don't stay the same

On the chart you will see that certain costs appear on the upper, wavy line. These costs are:

- **raw materials**
- **heating**
- **lighting**
- **stock**.

These costs are called **variable costs** because they increase as production increases. For example, if the shirt factory produces 5000 shirts instead of 2000, more raw materials will be used and so will cost more.

What do they mean?

- **Premises** = everything to do with the building rented or bought. This includes water and business rates, maintenance and repairs.

- **Equipment** = small and large items; from computers and vehicles to stationery.

- **Staff** = people who work for the business on a permanent or temporary basis. Their costs include wages, national insurance, pensions and holiday pay.

- **Advertising** = everything to do with promoting and selling the business' products and services, and recruiting staff.

- **Raw materials** = items which are used to make finished goods, or parts which are put together.

- **Stock** = goods or products for sale.

Case study

Yvonne's business costs

When Yvonne went to the bank to present her business plan to the branch manager, she had to take into consideration all the costs her business was likely to have.

Her weekly business costs might have been something like this:

<u>Yvonne's Flower Shop – weekly business costs</u>

Premises (including rent, business rates, water rates, fixtures and fittings) £180

Raw materials (dried and fresh flowers, ribbon and baskets) £200

Equipment (second-hand van, cold stores, till paper, till and so on) £110

Staff (wage for one trainee assistant) £65

Heating and lighting (mainly lighting the shop and window display. Flowers don't like to be too hot, so heating isn't too expensive). £20

Advertising (posters, leaflets and notices in local shops, houses, community centres and so on). £10

TOTAL **£585**

Of course this plan does not include cost of loans; money for tax, insurance and so on; or Yvonne's own salary.

Investigate costs and profit in business

Activity
Costs and outgoings

1 Look at the plan showing Yvonne's costs.
   a Which of Yvonne's costs are likely to be fixed? How much will she pay for them each week?
   b Which of Yvonne's costs are likely to be variable? How much is she paying for them now?
   c How can Yvonne reduce some of her business costs? List your ideas.
2 Think of the money you receive each week through any allowances, part-time work, pocket money and so on.
   a What fixed outgoings do you have (the same amount each week)?
   b What kinds of variable outgoings do you have (varying from week to week)?

How do employees contribute to business profit?

Once a business grows beyond being a small, sole trader with no employees, the workforce is one of its most valuable assets. Without a happy, willing workforce a company has little chance of being really successful.

Whilst a person's position in a company is important, it is not just the managing director who has an effect on a company's success. Everyone, even the most junior office assistant, has a worthwhile role in making a company efficient and profitable.

For more on employees, see page 109.

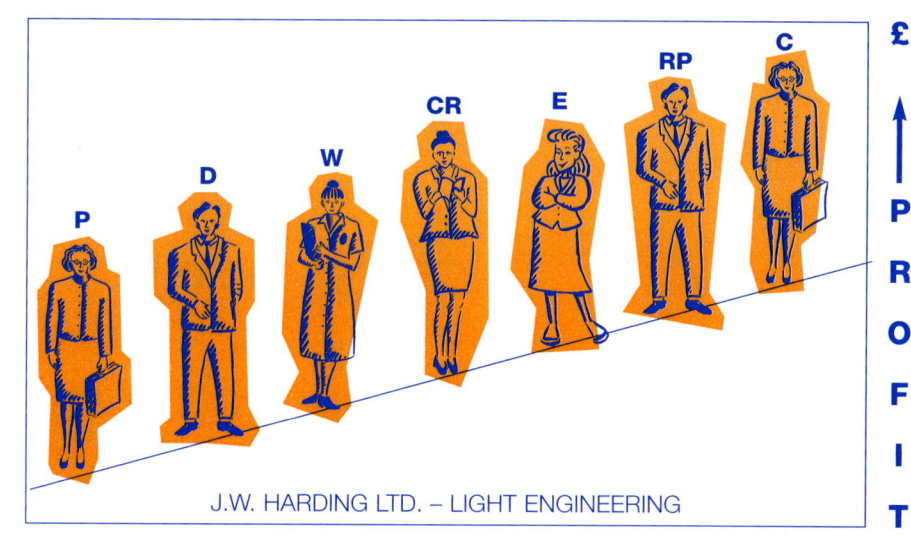

Key

P	= productivity
D	= working to deadlines
W	= reducing wastage
CR	= good customer relations
E	= reducing/eliminating errors
RP	= reporting problems
C	= communicating accurately

J.W. HARDING LTD. – LIGHT ENGINEERING

This chart shows the main areas in which employees can play an important part in helping to increase a company's profit. Everybody can do something about these areas in order to make themselves, and the company they work for, more profitable. It is up to the owners, directors, and managers to create the right kind of workplace: one which motivates workers to do well.

How to improve profitability

What do each of these ways of improving profitability involve?

Productivity
- Training workers and establishing good practice to make workers more productive.
- Making sure work is interesting and workers feel worthwhile so they produce more.
- Dividing work into sensible stages and tasks.
- Giving workers benefits for increased productivity.

'That's six machines we've finished today!'
'We used to only finish four'

Investigating business and customers

Working to deadlines
- Planning work and tasks carefully.
- Putting tasks in order of importance (the most important first).
- Allocating work fairly – one person can't do everything.
- Keeping check of progress.

'I've got three reports to do by 5pm. I'll do this one first, as it's for the boss and important'

Reducing wastage
- Making sure equipment is used properly.
- Making staff save energy – turning off unnecessary lights, machinery and so on.
- Telling staff how much money wastage can cost.
- Using time efficiently.
- Checking the use of materials.

'Can I help you?'

Good customer relations
- Being polite and friendly to customers.
- Answering customers' questions.
- Having good customer care services.
- Giving advice and information when asked for.
- Making a good impression.

'We make sure our staff are properly trained for their jobs and the tasks they must do'

Eliminating or reducing errors
- Encouraging staff to take a pride in their work.
- Making sure they are all properly trained to do their jobs.
- Providing up-to-date training and information.
- Having quality controls for goods produced.

Reporting problems
- Reporting small problems before they get bigger.
- Making sure staff feel able to talk to their bosses.
- Encouraging staff to look out for potential problems.
- Having plans for dealing with problems.

Communicating accurately
- Making sure memos, notes, reports and letters are written clearly and accurately.
- Having set forms for taking telephone messages and passing on information.
- Being honest when dealing with people in writing or by talking.

Activity
Increasing your own profitability

You could say that, as a student, you could increase your profitability by improving your success at studying and gaining qualifications. Using the categories for employee contributions to profit as a guide, make notes on how you could improve your own efficiency or 'profitability' as a student.

Interview someone in full-time employment to find out what steps their firm takes to improve efficiency and profitability. Record this interview on tape, and then write a report using the tape to remind yourself what they said.

For more on communication, see the Toolkit on page 8.

Investigate costs and profit in business

How can employees benefit from business profit?

Businesses can't expect their employees to work extra hard to increase profit without being rewarded in some way for doing so.

Often the chance to earn more money – in overtime or higher rates of pay – is enough of an encouragement for workers. However, there are other ways of rewarding them.

What are the main types of benefit?

'I helped introduce a scheme which increased my company's profits. So the boss asked me whether I wanted a bonus, some shares in the company, a part of the profits, or some other incentive. I chose a new company car.'

Share ownership
Workers employed by a public limited company may be given **shares** or allowed to buy them cheaply. They can then sell the shares if they wish, or receive their part of share profits as money twice a year.

Bonuses
Bonuses are usually extra money given as a reward for greater productivity. They are also given at particular times of the year; for example, Christmas and holiday-time.

Incentives
Incentives are also called **perks** or **fringe benefits**. They are another way of rewarding workers for new ideas, better working methods, increased profits and so on. They give employees a reason to work harder.

Incentives aren't part of a salary or wage, but are something extra, such as:
- company cars
- cheap loans for houses
- social facilities (sports clubs and so on)
- luncheon vouchers and cheap canteens
- free or cheap transport
- medical insurance
- cheap company goods or other discounts
- commission on goods or services sold.

What does it mean?

- **Shares** = people with shares in a company are part-owners, and get a share of the profits.

85

Investigating business and customers

Profit-sharing

For more on private and public limited companies see pages 105 and 106.

In public and private limited companies, usually once or twice a year, workers may be given a share of any profits their company makes as a percentage of their wage or salary. Profit-sharing makes workers feel part of the company when they cannot buy shares (for example, in a private limited company).

Activity

Matching benefits to staff

You are responsible for benefits to employees of your company. Which benefits – share ownership, bonuses, incentives or profit-sharing – would be best for:

1 a young person who has recently joined the company?
2 a salesperson?
3 a manager with a young family?
4 a middle-aged department manager?

Give reasons for your suggestions.

Activity (Application of Number)

Calculating profit

'Brollys' sells umbrellas. it is a section of a large department store.

During the year their profits change with the weather. During wet weather they sell many more umbrellas than when the sun shines. The table below shows the profits they made during the years 1991–1994. They are recorded every quarter (every 3 months).

Year	1991	1992	1993	1994
March	£228	£339	£380	£455
June	£157	£263	£294	£326
September	£89	£132	£145	£215
December	£362	£384	£473	£528

Use this information to draw a line graph to show Brollys' profits over the 4 years. Use a scale of 4 cm for each year (1 cm for each quarter) and 1 cm for each £20.

Comment on what your line graph shows. For example, when were the lowest points recorded? What is the general trend?

Answer the following questions.

1 How much profit did Brollys make in 1991?
2 What was the mean profit per month in 1991?
3 How much profit did Brollys make in 1994?
4 What was their mean profit per month in 1994?

For help calculating the mean, see the Toolkit on page 29.

To see what your graph should look like and for the answers, turn to page 100.

Raining? Don't get wet!
Get a "Brolly"!
COME TO 'BROLLYS' FOR A FINE RANGE OF UMBRELLAS

Investigate costs and profit in business

Assignment
Desktop

Setting the scene
You are a partner in a small company called 'Desktop', which sells office equipment. You have been quite successful in selling reconditioned second-hand computers and office furniture. You have one partner and employ three people.

You and your partner wish to expand the business by moving to larger premises on a new industrial estate. Most of your customers are other small businesses just setting up on their own.

Task 1
How would you and your partner go about raising the money needed for your plans?
- **a** List the main possible sources of money. What are the advantages and disadvantages of each?
- **b** List the reasons you want the loan.

Task 2
Another way to raise the extra money would be through a bank loan. To stand a good chance of obtaining the money you must provide the bank with a detailed list of your expected business costs in the new premises.

Write this list, making sure to include such things as costs of premises; additional equipment; extra wages for any additional staff; and any other expenses. (Look in the newspaper property ads for the cost of rental. Find out business rates for gas and electricity to help you determine costs.)

Task 3
Design:
- **a** a leaflet to distribute to firms on the industrial estate, telling them all about your business
- **b** an advertisement to place in the local paper, telling old and new customers about your move and what services/goods you offer.

Task 4
Find out how much it would cost you to:
- **a** have 200 leaflets printed by a firm in your area
- **b** advertise for a week in your local paper.

Task 5
You and your partner hold a meeting with your employees, telling them of your plans for the future of the business. You wish to impress upon them the importance of their contribution to the continued success of the company.

Make notes, for your own benefit, to prepare for the meeting.

Task 6
The meeting was very positive. Afterwards one of the staff asks you how they will benefit from all their efforts.

Explain the different kinds of benefits they could expect to receive if your company's profits continue to increase.

Opportunities to collect evidence

In this assignment you should cover:

Element 2.2
- PC1
- PC2
- PC3
- PC4

Application of Number
- Element 1.2

Communication
- Element 1.1
- Element 1.2
- Element 1.3
- Element 1.4

Information Technology (if work is word processed)
- Element 1.1
- Element 1.2
- Element 1.3

Investigating business and customers

❓ Quiz

See page 134 for the answers.

How much do you know about costs and profits?

1. Young people preferring Dr Marten shoes to sandals is an example of:
   a business costs
   b competition
   c customer preference
   d management

2. A factory making jeans increases its production from 2000 to 2500 pairs a week without increasing costs. This is an example of increasing:
   a customer preference
   b competition
   c business costs
   d productivity

3. A fish and chip shop owner discovers that another take-away shop is opening in the next road. This is an example of increased competition for the fish and chip shop. True or False?

4. The owners of a small printing firm have failed to plan for the time when they will need to buy new machinery. This is an example of not managing the business properly. True or False?

5. Two young people plan to open a hairdresser's shop in their local shopping centre. They plan to rent a shop as they cannot afford to buy one. Which example of business costs is this?
   a staff
   b premises
   c equipment
   d raw materials

6. The same two people must buy chairs, driers, mirrors and so on for their shop. This cost is an example of spending money on:
   a premises
   b raw materials
   c equipment
   d advertising

7. A new estate agent decides to have leaflets printed, telling people what it offers. Which of the following types of business costs is this?
   a equipment
   b heating
   c staff
   d advertising

8. The sales team had problems promoting a new product, but were able to talk to their manager about it and find solutions. Which of the following employee contributions was this?
   a working to deadlines
   b good customer relations
   c reporting problems
   d reducing wastage

9. When employees finish tasks on time they are making the following contribution:
   a reporting problems
   b working to deadlines
   c communicating accurately
   d productivity

10. A factory which had an increase in profit gave its workers extra money in their pay-packets. Which benefit is this an example of?
    a share ownership
    b bonus
    c profit-sharing
    d incentives

Scoring

If you scored:
- between 1 and 4 – your knowledge of the factors which influence costs and profits is a little shaky! You should re-read this section and ask your tutor for help.
- between 5 and 7 – your understanding of this element is reasonable. Perhaps you are uncertain about one or two performance criteria.
- 8 and above – well done! You obviously understand the ideas contained in this section about how a business' profits increase or decrease and why this can happen.

Make a sales presentation to a customer

In this element you will learn how to make a successful sales presentation – what to include and what to avoid doing. You will also have the opportunity to make your own presentation and to assess how well it went.

By the end of this element you should be able to:

- describe the stages in the selling process
- explain clearly the features of a product to a potential customer
- answer clearly any questions which the customer may ask about the product
- communicate clearly the intention to sell the product
- assess the effectiveness of the sales presentation.

What is a sales presentation?

'Good morning everyone. My name is Helen Anderson'

A sales presentation is one of the ways a company can promote a product, idea or service.

It is not promotion on such a large scale as advertising, but it can be a very effective way of getting customers to know about your product. One person or a small team usually makes a presentation, and it may be done to as small an audience as one customer. Its purpose is to encourage the customer to buy the product, service or idea. It's rather like an interview for a job; but instead of selling yourself, you are selling your company's product. When you make a presentation you must convince a particular customer that what you are selling is worth buying, as it's the best of its kind. How can you do this?

1 By understanding the process involved in selling a product or service.
2 By knowing everything there is to know about the product.
3 By being able to answer any questions which the customer might ask.
4 By being a good, convincing sales presenter.

Presentations happen when:
- a range of goods or a product is introduced to a new customer
- a new product is introduced to an old customer
- a new idea is introduced to other members of the same company
- a door-to-door salesperson shows samples and gives information to customers
- goods are presented at trade fairs and exhibitions to other companies.

For more on making a presentation, see the Toolkit on page 9.

Investigating business and customers

Stages in the selling process

'I'm Regional Sales Manager for Harper Tools, a company which manufactures and supplies general-purpose tools to DIY stores and garden centres. It's my responsibility to make sure all my sales representatives are fully trained in the process of selling our products. At our regular sales training sessions we talk about the following points.

- **Introduction/greeting.** Sales representatives must always greet customers cheerfully and politely. They must always know the customer's name, introduce themselves by name, and mention the company. 
- **Finding out the customer's needs.** It's no good trying to sell products to a customer who already has them or will never need them. Sales reps should carry stock lists, brochures and product information to show the customer. They shouldn't hesitate to find out which products are successful and which are not.
- **Presentation of the product.** Sales reps should demonstrate both new products, and established products which may be new to the customer. They should make sure they know all the products well.
- **Countering objections.** Sales reps must be prepared to answer any questions, queries and objections a customer may raise about a product. They must put the customer's mind at ease about quality, payment, competitiveness, safety and so on.
- **Closing the sale.** Sales reps will know through experience when the time is right to make the sale. Customers must never be rushed into making a purchase. They must be given time to make up their minds.

'Hello Mr. Jones. I'm Miss Bloom from Harper Tools. How is everything?'

'Have you decided how many to have?'

'I'll take five boxes.'

- **After-sales follow-up.** A good sales rep will make return visits or phone calls to check whether the product has been delivered safely and whether it has matched the customer's needs and expectations.'

What do they mean?

- **Sales rep** = someone responsible for selling goods or services to customers. 'Rep' is short for 'representative' – the sales rep is a representative of the firm.
- **Countering objections** = to give opinions and ideas that answer any criticisms or difficult questions.

Make a sales presentation to a customer

Knowing the product

Sales presentations might not be necessary if customers didn't have such a wide range of products from which to choose. Because there is so much choice, companies are in **competition** with each other to sell their products. In order to do this they must bring their products to the attention of as many possible customers as they can. A sales presentation is one way of doing this.

When you make a presentation you need to give the customer as much information as possible. You must convince the customer to buy your product above all others. Much of the information the customer needs to know will be about a product's **features**.

These features will include:
- what the product does (its purpose)
- how to use it
- how much it costs (to buy and perhaps to run)
- what it has that other products don't have (its **unique selling point**).

'Our windows are the best…'

Presenters must be able to say why their product is the best

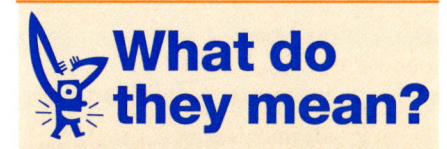

What information would customers want to know about the features of the products shown here?

What do they mean?

- **Competition** = when several companies are trying to sell the same goods or services, they compete for customers.

- **Unique selling point** = what makes a product stand out from others available – why the customer should buy it. 'Unique selling point' is often shortened to 'USP'.

Here is an example of a product which might interest someone who likes watching TV in bed!

Price
Only £490 – a bargain as you get two machines for the price of one!

Purpose
To entertain you. Now you can watch TV or videos in bed using one piece of equipment.

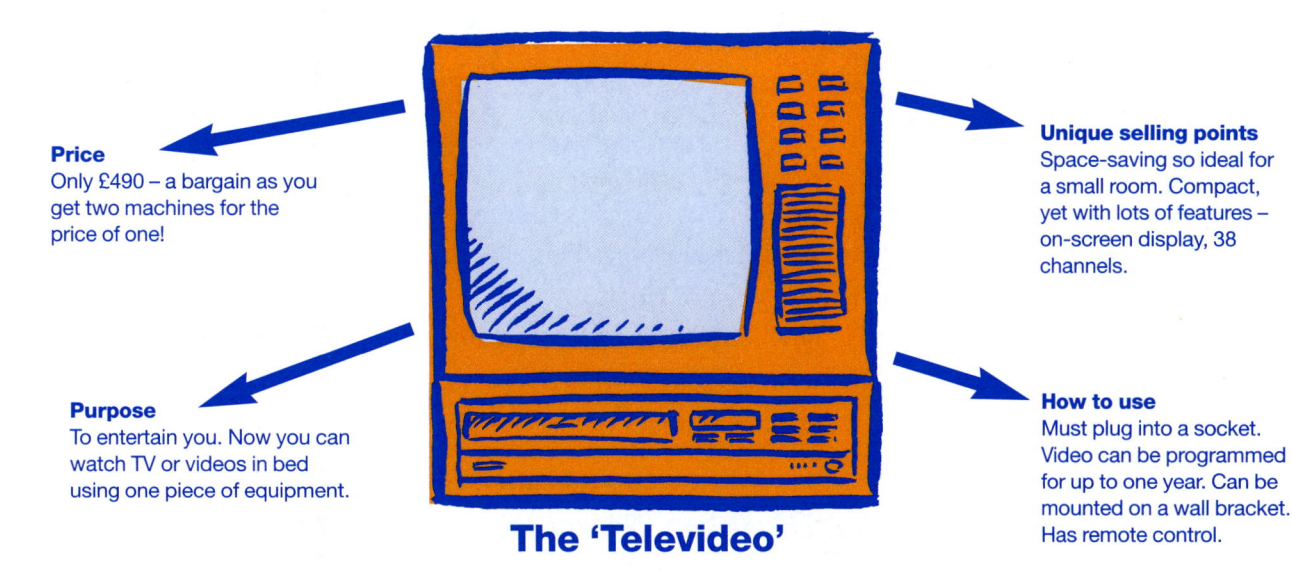

Unique selling points
Space-saving so ideal for a small room. Compact, yet with lots of features – on-screen display, 38 channels.

How to use
Must plug into a socket. Video can be programmed for up to one year. Can be mounted on a wall bracket. Has remote control.

The 'Televideo'

Investigating business and customers

Activity
Product knowledge

1. Select a product that you own and that you know quite a lot about. Explain its main features to a member of your group. Then ask that person to repeat the information back to you. How much did he or she manage to take in?
2. Select two products you might buy. They should be nearly the same price and serve the same purpose; for example, two pairs of trainers. What would make you choose one pair rather than the other? Would any of the points mentioned before influence you? (Purpose, use, cost, uniqueness.) Write up your views in a short report; mentioning products chosen, reason(s) for selection, and features which influenced you most.
3. Ask someone in your house about a product they have recently bought (this could be anything from washing-up liquid to a new car). Find out how much they know about its features, and which influenced them the most when buying.

Answering questions about the product

If you were about to buy a new jacket, you would probably ask yourself certain questions before you took it to a cash till.

- How can I pay for this?
- Is it worth the money?
- Can I bring it back if necessary?
- Does it suit me?
- Can I afford it?
- Does it fit?
- Is the shop a good one with which to do business?
- Will it go with what I have already?
- Is the fabric flammable?
- Are the materials and dyes safe to wear?

If the answers to these questions were satisfactory, you would probably buy the jacket. The salesperson will answer some of these questions; for example, 'How can I pay for it?' and 'What happens if it's faulty?'

The more complicated or expensive the product, the more questions you are likely to want answered before you part with your money.

Buying from a shop

'Can I help you?'
'Yes. Can I use my credit card?'

Ask someone who works there

Buying from a company

'Any questions?'
'Yes. What will it cost to service?'
'What about payment?'

Ask the person making the presentation

Apart from asking questions about a product's features, a customer is also likely to want to know:

- how the product can be bought (payment)
- what after-sales service is provided
- what guarantees (if any) are given.

You are about to spend a lot of money on a new mini stereo system. What questions will you ask the sales assistant?

Make a sales presentation to a customer

Ways of paying

In Unit 1 we looked at different ways of paying for something.

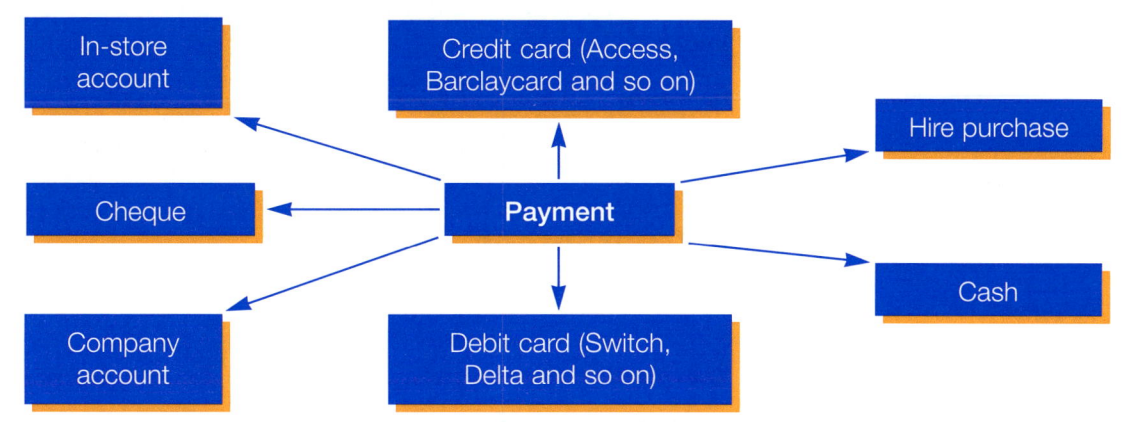

```
In-store account
Cheque
Company account
Credit card (Access, Barclaycard and so on)
Payment
Debit card (Switch, Delta and so on)
Hire purchase
Cash
```

For more on ways of paying, see page 37.

The way you pay for something will often depend on what you buy and where you buy it; for example:

- some companies will accept cash, cheques and debit cards, but not credit cards
- some companies will not accept cheques above a certain level, but will accept credit cards.

So it is important to ask how you can pay for something.

Activity
Ways of paying – a mini-survey

Conduct a mini-survey at your local shopping centre to find out how people can pay for goods and services at eight to ten different shops. You may find it useful to produce a 'data collection sheet', with the names of shops down the side and different payment methods along the top. You can then tick which payment methods are accepted quickly and easily.

Some of the information you need will be clearly shown in shop windows or doors (for example, whether you can pay by credit card). Some information you will have to find out by politely asking shopkeepers what methods they accept.

Use your information to draw a bar chart, showing the number of payment methods on one axis and the number of shops on the other.

For more on drawing bar charts, see the Toolkit on page 18.

After-sales service

When you buy something, especially if it is expensive, you need to know that the company selling it to you provides an after-sales service. If something goes wrong with it, if it is faulty, or if you don't understand how something works, the company should be able to help you. Different companies will have different ways of providing this service. So it's important to ask what kind of service they offer!

'What's the problem'

'It won't work!'

- Advice (what help they provide)
- Information (about goods and so on)
- Refunds, credits and exchanges
- Repairs and servicing
- Making sure goods are 'fit for their purpose'
- Complaints (how and when to complain)

93

Investigating business and customers

> ### Activity
> **After-sales service for a car**
> A car is an expensive product to buy, and it is important it is cared for properly.
> Ask someone you know who owns a car what after-sales services were provided by the garage which sold it. (You might also like to ask them how they paid for it.) Make a note of their reply and compare it with the information gathered by other students in your group.

Guarantees

You could say that a **guarantee** is part of a company's after-sales service, as it is something it promises to do after a product has been sold.

- A guarantee is a written promise, given by a company, to replace any faulty parts or goods if they go wrong within a certain time. The promise will only be carried out if the product has been used correctly and treated properly.
- A guarantee is usually good for a set time only; for example, one year for most small electrical goods.
- In order for the guarantee to be of any use, you must keep your receipt and fill in a guarantee slip for the company. This is your **proof of purchase**.

Guarantee
Your Aquabright bathroom suite is guaranteed for 15 years. In order to ensure your rights to under guarantee service aren't affected, please complete this form at the time of purchase and present it to the dealer as a guarantee.

Surname: Azad
Forenames: Sherin
Address: 24 Appleby Way, Woodley, Notts DN18 3YU
Name of suite: Cranleigh
Date of sale: 28/6/95
Purchased from: Better Bathrooms, Kingsford
Order number: BB 32170

For more on proof of purchase, see page 54.

> ### Activity
> **Investigating a product you wish to buy**
> Now that you know what types of important information you need before buying a product, complete the following activity as preparation for the assignment at the end of this element.
> 1. Select a product you would like to buy in the near future. Say what it is, where you would buy it, and its price.
> 2. Describe the main features of the product.
> 3. Find out from the shop the methods of payment you would be able to use.
> 4. What after-sales service is offered for the product?
> 5. If the product has a guarantee, how long is it for and are there any conditions with it?
>
> Write down your results as a report for the rest of the group.

Making a presentation to sell a product

For more on job roles, see page 109.

If your **job role** in a company is to make sales presentations, no matter how small, you make a valuable contribution to your company's success.

Successful presentations mean higher sales figures and higher profits for the company. It is important that anyone whose job it is to make presentations does them as effectively as possible.

When you make a presentation you represent your company. The impression you make on your audience will help decide what they think of the product you are trying to sell.

To them, a sloppy presentation might mean a 'sloppy' product.

Make a sales presentation to a customer

Practice makes perfect...

The first time...

The second time...

The third time...

The fourth time...

Case study
The tale of the first-time presenter

'I'll never forget the first time I had to make a presentation for my office equipment company. I had to introduce a new stapler to a small printing company. Everything that could have gone wrong did go wrong. I thought I knew where the firm was, didn't take the map and got lost on the industrial estate. I eventually arrived, hot and flustered, fifteen minutes late. I was nervous, sweating and looking a mess. Not a good start!

I had prepared notes, but dropped them in the car park. I picked them up in the wrong order, covered in mud. I finally reported to reception, was shown in to the director's room, dropped my notes again and then realised I'd left the stapler back at my firm! I can laugh about it now...'

An effective presentation

Make sure you prepare well

- Really know the product you are selling.
- Make notes and prepare any visual aids you might need (charts, diagrams and so on).
- Find out how big your audience will be, who will be there, and what their positions are in the company.
- Rehearse and time your presentation.
- Try to memorise your introduction and use notes for the rest.

95

Investigating business and customers

What do they mean?

- **Body language** = the way you communicate using your body; for example, the way you stand, sit, move your hands.
- **Jargon** = words and technical terms that other people might not understand.

For more on body language, see the Toolkit on page 11.

The presentation: the 10-point plan

1 Be sure to introduce yourself.
2 Smile and don't worry if you are nervous – that will be expected and understood.
3 Seem confident but **not** cocky.
4 Take two or three deep breaths before you start, to help you keep calm.
5 Say what you are going to talk about – the introduction.
6 Go over each point you mentioned in the introduction.
7 Use a polite and friendly tone of voice.
8 Use positive **body language** – look at your audience not at the floor; stand up straight, but not tense.
9 Keep language straightforward; don't use **jargon**.
10 Look smart.

You will know your presentation is good if…

- You dressed smartly, but not over the top.
- You spoke clearly and at just the right speed – not too fast, nor too slow.
- You didn't shuffle notes too much or make too many nervous gestures (fiddling with hair, and so on).
- Your audience didn't fidget, look bored or stare out the window.
- You tried to get variety into your voice.
- You used notes and kept to them; not waffling or straying from the point.
- You checked whether any equipment you needed was there and working.
- You added some humour to your talk.
- Your audience asked sensible and relevant questions which you **could** answer.
- They bought the product!

You will know your presentation is poor if…

- You didn't know the essential information about your product.
- You hadn't planned your presentation properly.
- You waffled and lost your way in your presentation.
- You didn't speak clearly – perhaps mumbling or speaking too quickly.
- You gave too much information in too short a time.
- Your charts and diagrams were muddled, and you didn't check any necessary equipment.
- Your audience looked bored, yawned, fidgeted…
- Your body language was wrong – you slouched and avoided looking at your audience.
- You fidgeted and looked sloppy.
- You couldn't answer the questions which were asked.
- They **didn't** buy the product!

Make a sales presentation to a customer

Activity
Summer holidays – a short talk

As preparation for the assignment at the end of this element, prepare a short talk for your group. Your subject should be a suitable summer holiday for young people. You may have to visit your local travel agent to collect information about the holiday's features, price and so on. You must give reasons for your choice. Ask for honest and positive comments about the talk (the content, your body language and your voice).

If possible, record the talk on a video and play it back. Note your strengths and weaknesses. Then try again, record the presentation, and note improvements.

Assessing your presentation

In the world of business, poor sales presentations for a product normally mean poor sales. Poor sales figures would be one way of assessing customer response. Unless you were completely unaware of your audience, you would have a good idea of customers' reactions just by looking at them.

Body language is important to remember; not only for your own performance, but also for judging how your audience is reacting to you.

The following checklist may help you judge your audience's response to your presentation. You can photocopy it and complete it after a presentation.

Questions to ask yourself		
Positive responses	Yes	No
Did your audience look at you most of the time? (good eye contact)		
Did they seem alert and interested; leaning forward, perhaps nodding? (good body language)		
Did they ask relevant questions which were straightforward?		
Did they thank you at the end of the presentation?		
Negative responses	Yes	No
Did your audience fidget, seem restless, yawn and frown? (poor body language)		
Did they avoid looking at you? (poor eye contact)		
Did they look bored or talk among themselves?		
Did they ask only awkward questions, if any?		

Positive or negative?

For more ideas on communicating well, see the Toolkit on page 8.

Foundation GNVQ Business © Murphy and Palmer, 1995.
Published by Thomas Nelson & Sons Ltd.

Investigating business and customers

You can also get members of the group to assess each other when you make your presentations.

Photocopy the form on the right and try using it for this type of assessment. It should be honestly and positively completed.

Name of presenter ....
Name of assessor ....
Product/subject ....
Tick the correct column (3 is very good, 1 is not very good)

	3	2	1
Presentation • preparation (notes etc.) • knowledge of product/subject • organisation of presentation • introduction • coverage of main points • interest			
Visual aids (if used) • suitability • did they add to your knowledge of the product?			
Delivery • appearance (smart/sloppy) • enthusiasm for product • body language • eye contact • mannerisms • confidence			
Voice • pace and tone • could you follow what was said?			
Questions • did they show knowledge of the product/subject?			

Assignment

Making your first sales presentation

Setting the scene

You are a junior member of the sales department of a local company.

You have been asked to prepare a short presentation to introduce one of your company's best selling products to a new customer. The sales manager tells you that you should also prepare a brief hand-out to give to the customer. The hand-out must include all the important information contained in your presentation. The essential information is:

- the company name and logo (you choose)
- the name of the product
- the main features of the product
- its price and how customers can pay
- after-sales service and guarantees provided by your company.

You may choose a product you know quite a lot about, or you may decide to invent a product.

Task 1
List the stages you will go through in order to sell your product or services.

Task 2
After you have chosen your product, prepare notes for the presentation. Remember, you should write the introduction in full, as you might find it easier to read this before referring to your notes. Prepare any charts, pictures or diagrams you need.

Task 3
Using the information you prepared for your presentation, produce the customer hand-out.

It should be straightforward, to the point and contain the main points about your product.

You should word process the hand-out, so it looks professional and realistic.

Task 4
Give your presentation to the rest of the group. When you have finished, the assessment forms on pages 97 and 98 should be completed – one by you, and one by the others in the group.

Task 5
Write a summary of your performance in the presentation and how well you think you did.

Opportunities to collect evidence

In this assignment you should cover:

Element 2.3
PC1
PC2
PC3
PC4

Communication
Element 1.1
Element 1.2
Element 1.3
Element 1.4

Information Technology
Element 1.1
Element 1.2
Element 1.3

Application of Number
Element 1.2

Foundation GNVQ Business © Murphy and Palmer, 1995.
Published by Thomas Nelson & Sons Ltd.

❓ Quiz

How good are you at sales presentations?

See page 134 for the answers.

1. A customer wants to buy a new lawnmower. Which **one** of the following is the **most** important feature of the lawnmower?
   - **a** it comes with lots of gadgets
   - **b** it is the right one for the purpose – to cut grass
   - **c** it is attractive to look at
   - **d** it is reduced in price in a sale

2. Someone who wants to buy a microwave for the first time will find **one** of the following features **most** important:
   - **a** easy to understand instructions
   - **b** the price
   - **c** the colour
   - **d** it is advertised on TV

3. A new type of running shoe is the only one to be made of a special washable material. This feature is known as:
   - **a** its price
   - **b** its unique selling point
   - **c** its usefulness
   - **d** its novelty

4. A TV set is on sale in a department store. It is £100 cheaper than a similar set sold in another store. Which **one** of the following features is **most** likely to attract a customer?
   - **a** free delivery
   - **b** easy to use instructions
   - **c** style
   - **d** price

5. Which **one** of the following is **most** important to have when buying an expensive stereo system?
   - **a** a choice of colours
   - **b** a guarantee on parts and repairs
   - **c** remote control
   - **d** extra long leads

6. A customer wanting to buy a new car needs to know:
   - **a** the name of the garage owner
   - **b** the different methods of paying for it
   - **c** that it won an award for best car
   - **d** that it is a new type of model

7. A company offering to repair or replace faulty goods bought from them is providing:
   - **a** fast delivery
   - **b** an after-sales service
   - **c** competitive rates
   - **d** different ways of paying

Scoring

If you scored:

- 1 or 2 – you need to know more about the features of products and the questions asked about them. You should re-read this section.
- 3 or 4 – you have a reasonable understanding of the points covered in this section, but be sure to check those points which you got wrong.
- 5 and above – you have a good understanding of the kinds of information needed to make a successful sales presentation.

Investigating business and customers

Answers

p.69 They are all types of business. They might exist for different reasons, but they are all businesses.

p.73 Activity – What do you know?

1 False 2 True 3 True 4 True 5 False
6 False 7 True 8 False 9 False 10 False
11 True 12 True 13 True

p.85 Activity – calculating profit

1 £836
2 £209
3 £1524
4 £381

Brollys' profits 1991–1994

PROFIT (£)

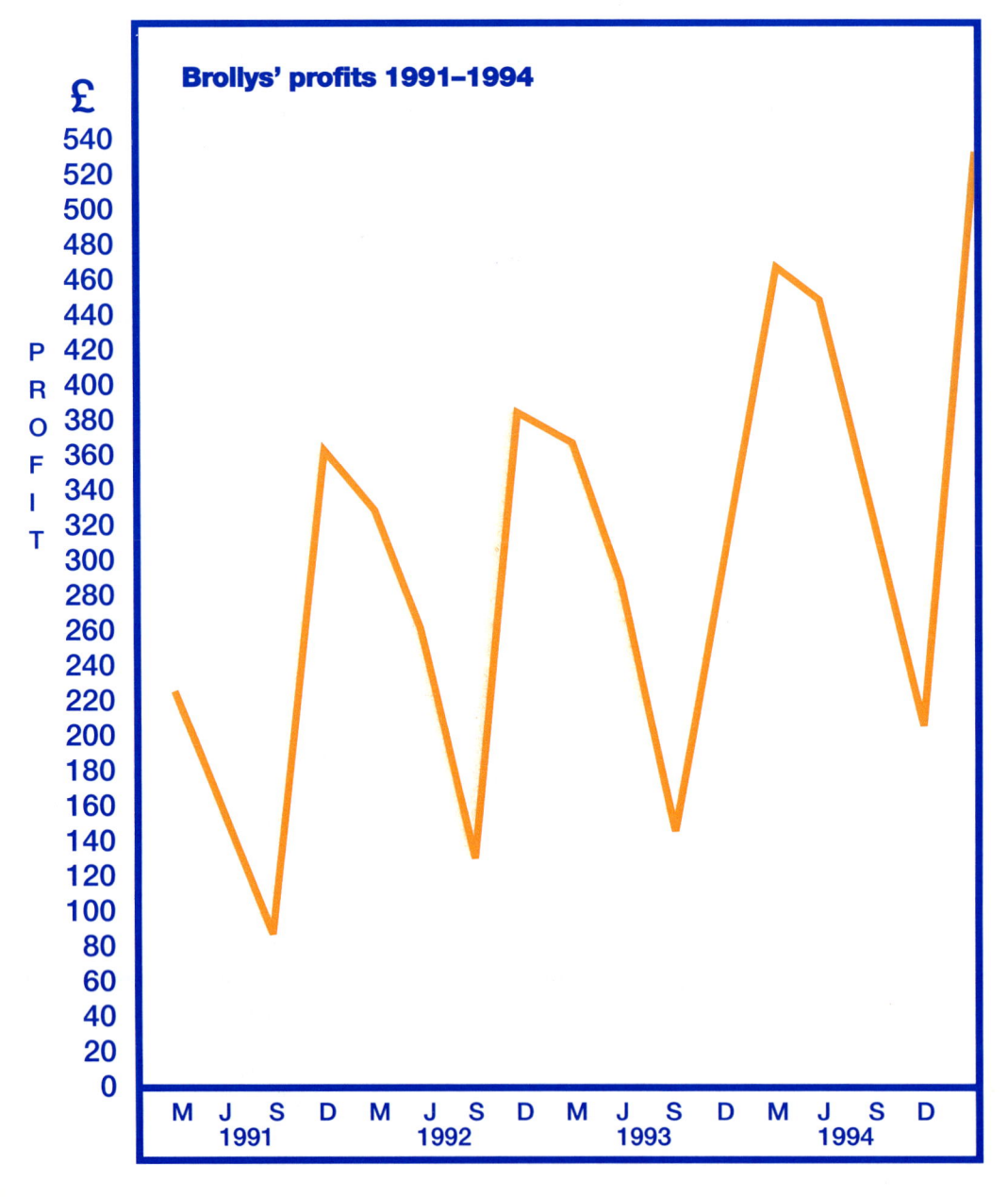

x-axis: M J S D M J S D M J S D M J S D
        1991   1992   1993   1994

Line shows:
Lowest points were recorded in September (this quarter includes the summer). The general trend is constantly upwards. December and March are both good quarters.
(Not to scale)

Unit 3
Investigating working in business

Introduction

This unit focuses on the opportunities for employment in business. It also looks at the purposes of different jobs, and the skills and qualifications you need to do them. This unit will help you to:

- explore types of business organisation and personnel in departments
- investigate jobs in business
- plan for employment in business.

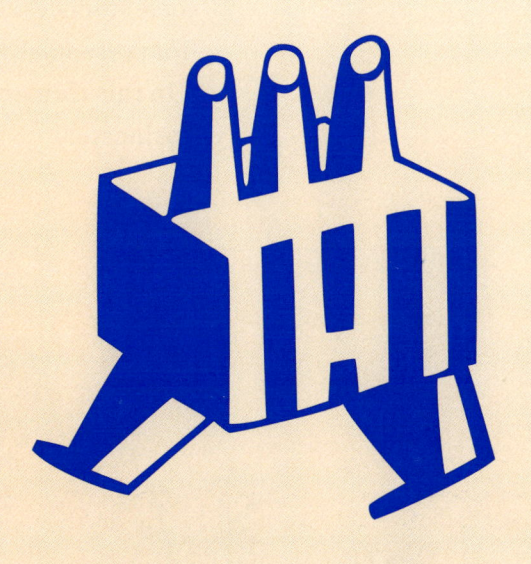

Investigating working in business

Business organisations and personnel in departments

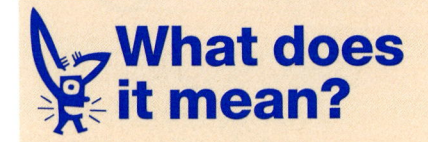

What does it mean?
- **Personnel = people who work in an organisation.**

This element looks at different types of business organisations; the people who work in them; and the responsibilities which go with their jobs. This information might help you decide what area of business interests you – perhaps for a job once you have finished studying.

By the end of this element you should be able to:
- identify and give examples of types of business organisations
- identify the departments generally found in large business organisations and their purpose
- identify job titles of personnel in business organisations
- describe the areas of responsibility which go with the job titles in departments.

Types of business organisations – who owns what?

For more on purposes of businesses, see page 68.

For more on goods and services, see page 72.

When you investigated the **purposes** of different businesses in your local area, you may also have noticed the different **types** of businesses there were. Businesses in Britain are either privately or publicly owned – in the **private sector**, or the **public sector**.

Both sectors produce **goods** and **services** we like to have in our society. However, most of the goods and services provided for people in Britain come from businesses which are privately owned. These businesses range from very small firms to immensely large companies.

In this element we will look at the following types of privately-owned businesses:

Sole Trader   Partnership   Franchise   Private Limited Company   Public Limited Company

Remember: all of these businesses must make a profit to survive

Business organisations and personnel in departments

Sole trader – be your own boss

Lots of people set up in business on their own. They do so for a number of reasons: to be their own boss; to invest their redundancy money; or to do something they've always wanted to. These people are known as **sole traders** – they are doing business on their own. Sole traders not only own the business, they must take responsibility for it. They may employ other people to work for them, but they remain the boss. This type of business is usually small in size – often hairdressers, cafés and general shops are sole traders.

Advantages
- You are your own boss.
- It's a simple business to start.
- You don't have to work with partners – you make all the decisions.
- You may not need much money to start.
- You get to keep all the profit.
- You can offer a personal service.
- You can work when you want.

Disadvantages
- You may have problems if you can't run your business for any reason, as only you know about it.
- It's harder to borrow money for improving or expanding.
- You may have to work hard and for very long hours.
- Your product or service may be more expensive than a big company's.
- You're responsible for all your business' losses.
- You could be made bankrupt.

Activity
Being self-employed

Do you know anyone who is in business on their own?

If you do, ask them what the good and bad things are about working for themselves.

Case study
Paula is a success, could you be?

Paula Jones, aged 20

'I took advantage of a government 'Start-Up' scheme for young people who want to work for themselves. I had assistance and advice from the local government office about grants and so on. I now run a mobile indoor landscape business. I look after plants for companies and hotels. I have two vans now. It is hard work but I love being my own boss.'

If you could be your own boss and set up in business on your own, what would you do? Why?

Investigating working in business

Partnerships – two heads are better than one

Sometimes people find it best to work with others; just as sometimes it is easier to complete activities if you are part of a team. It is the same in business.

A **business partnership** is when two or more people (usually no more than twenty) decide to work together in a team. In this way they can share their skills, expertise and experience in order to make a profit. When you work as a partner you share the responsibility of running your business with your partner, or other partners. People like lawyers, dentists, surveyors, architects and accountants often work in partnership with each other.

So that each person knows what to expect from the partnership, a document called a Deed of Partnership is often made between the partners. This document is usually drawn up by a solicitor. It includes the following types of information.

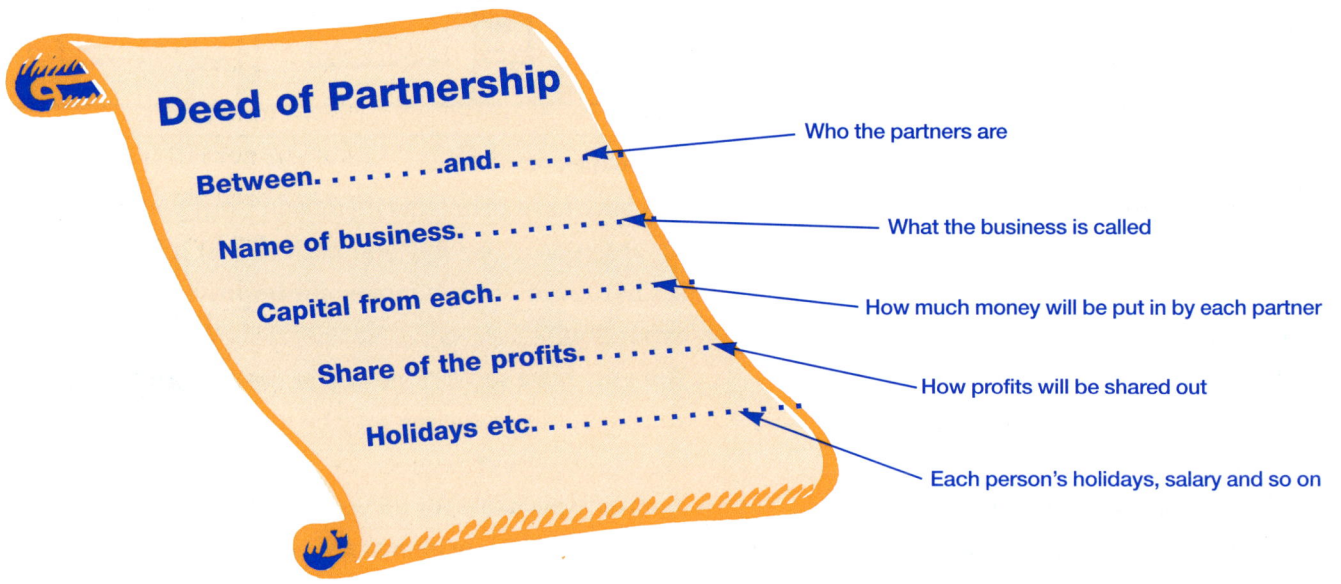

Deed of Partnership

- Between. . . . . . . .and. . . . . — Who the partners are
- Name of business. . . . . — What the business is called
- Capital from each. . . . . — How much money will be put in by each partner
- Share of the profits. . . . . . . — How profits will be shared out
- Holidays etc. . . . . — Each person's holidays, salary and so on

Advantages
- Responsibilities and problems are shared.
- There's greater scope for borrowing money.
- It is easier to specialise in different areas.
- Partnerships can provide a wider service.
- Partners bring money and different skills to the business.
- It is easier to take holidays.

Disadvantages
- Each partner is responsible for the losses if any – they could all be made bankrupt.
- Each partner has to rely on the others working hard and honestly.
- Partners may disagree how to run the business.
- The partnership could end if something happens to a partner.

Activity
Partnerships – how can you tell?
Look in the *Yellow Pages* under Solicitors, Accountants and Dentists. Write down the names of ten firms you think are partnerships. Can you tell by the names of businesses whether or not they are partnerships?

Business organisations and personnel in departments

Private limited companies – 'up and coming'

Being a partnership can have advantages over being a sole trader, but if anything goes wrong the partners are still **liable** for all the business' debts.

If a business is likely to have high outgoings – because it has to buy expensive equipment or materials, rent or buy a building, or doesn't get paid quickly by its customers – it is best for the business to become a **private limited company**.

When a business becomes a private limited company, the owners are not personally liable for the debts of the business. If the worst came to the worst, they would not lose their own possessions (for example, their homes).

If a business wishes to become a private limited company, it must:
- complete various documents for the **Registrar of Companies**
- keep its accounts and record books in good order, so that they can be looked at/checked every year by the Registrar of Companies.

People who own a limited company are called **shareholders**. You can tell if a business is a private limited company by the letters **Ltd.** after its name.

For more about shares, see page 85.

What do they mean?

- **To be liable** = you are responsible for something – even if this causes you to lose out. In business this responsibility can be for money or goods owed. Sole traders and partnerships have unlimited liability. This means there is no limit to the amount they might have to pay if they owe money in business.

- **The Registrar of Companies** = the government office that keeps records of all companies in the UK.

Advantages
- If the company runs into trouble, the owners, or shareholders, can only lose the amount of money they invested.
- Other people can become part-owners or shareholders by buying shares in the company.
- Money can be raised by selling shares or taking out a loan.
- The business can grow and develop by raising more money.

Disadvantages
- Shares can only be sold to family and friends.
- You cannot own a limited company on your own.
- You might fall out with other shareholders.
- You must keep your accounts and other records in good order.

Activity
Limited companies

Visit your local industrial estate, business park or shopping centre to find companies which have Ltd. after their names. Try to do this as part of another activity in this book, as the information will be useful for other tasks.

Make a list of the companies and say what type of business each is. Take photographs of some of the limited companies you found and make a small display.

Investigating working in business

Public limited company – the premier division

Some businesses stay small; other companies grow and grow and grow. When a company grows it expands. When a company expands it hopes to:
- make larger profits for its shareholders (owners)
- produce more of the same goods/services
- produce a greater variety of goods/services
- be the best at what it does
- increase its share of the market (sell more products).

In order to expand a company needs money (capital). One of the easiest ways of raising money is to sell more shares.

If it is a private limited company, it can only sell its shares to family and friends.

But if a company 'goes public', it can sell its shares to anyone who has the money to buy them. Of course, there are many rules and regulations companies have to follow when they go public.

A company must have at least £50,000 capital, and must spend money on solicitor's fees, advertising for shareholders and so on. So not all private limited companies want, or can afford, to go public. **A public limited company** must also produce accounts for everyone to see and must tell its shareholders how money has been spent.

What does it mean?

- plc = public limited company. All public limited companies must have these letters after their names.

Activity
The pros and cons of going public

Copy the following table, and using the information above fill in three advantages and three disadvantages of being a public limited company.

Advantages	Disadvantages
1.	1.
2.	2.
3.	3.

Activity
Famous plcs – what do they provide?

Because of their size, many public limited companies are well-known names – you probably know many. Select one well-known plc and research ten different products or services it provides. Comment on how easy it was to gather this information.

For help with your research, see the Toolkit on page 4.

Case study
Filofax – 'wonder of the 80s: success of the 90s'

Filofax Group plc, the company which makes personal organisers, is an example of a modern company which has expanded rapidly in recent years. It has grown from a small company, producing one item, into a public limited company which buys up other companies. It now produces many different kinds of diaries, calendars and paper products.

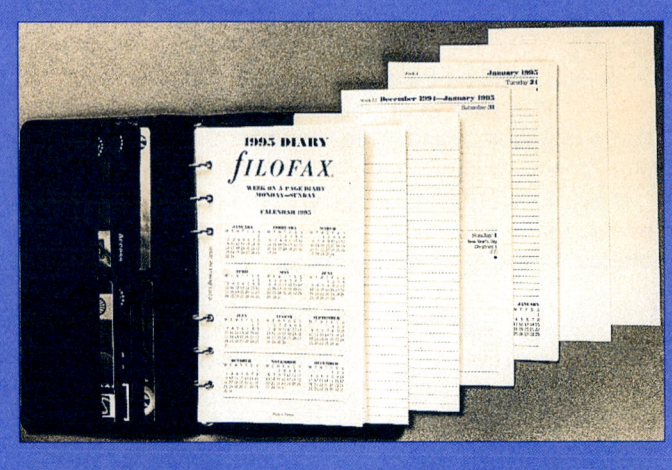

106

Business organisations and personnel in departments

Franchise – a small part of a bigger whole

Franchises are becoming popular in Britain, and you can see examples in most shopping centres. If you recognise the names Body Shop, Pizza Hut, Prontaprint, Burger King and Tie Rack, you already know five examples of franchises.

Franchises are run by people who have bought the right to sell the products or services, and to use the name, logo and reputation of a large, well-known company. They are not managers or partners. They buy or rent their building, and they must have capital to put into the franchise. They must sell the products or services in the way the company says; but they receive advice and get to keep most of the profits.

Co-operatives – working together

Co-operatives are quite a common form of business organisation in the United Kingdom. They are called 'co-operatives' because the workers decide to co-operate at all levels to run a business on their own.

Many co-operatives come about when workers buy the organisation where they work from its original owners. In a co-operative:
- workers own a share of the organisation – they are paid a salary or wage **and** a share of the profits
- there are no limits on how many people may belong
- a certain amount of profit is put back into the organisation.

Co-operatives can be limited companies, but their shares do not rise in value. If one owner decides to sell shares, the shares can only be bought by another member of the co-operative.

Local authority services

The businesses we have looked at so far are all in the **private sector**. In our communities there are other organisations which provide us with a wide range of services – free of charge, or sometimes for a charge. These organisations are part of the **public sector**.

Communities in Britain are organised into large regions and smaller districts. These are known as **local authorities**.

It is the local authorities who are responsible for supplying their residents with certain essential services – including education, social services, fire services, refuse collection and libraries.

These services make a big difference to people's lives. When the refuse collectors went on strike a few years ago, the mountains of uncollected rubbish were definitely neither pleasant nor healthy!

Some local authority services are now performed by private firms, who have won contracts from local authorities. Although the work is done by the private companies, the local authority is still responsible for them.

Activity
Examples of franchises
What other examples of franchises do you know? List them, and say what they sell or provide.

Case study
British School of Motoring (BSM)
BSM is the largest franchisor of driving tuition for learner drivers in the UK, operating through 150 high street branches. BSM instructors enjoy the advantages of being self-employed while benefiting from the support of a large, well-established organisation. In return for a weekly franchise fee, BSM instructors receive a support package which includes a maintained Vauxhall Corsa tuition car, a regular supply of pupils, marketing support, advertising, and accident and sickness insurance.

Activity
What local authorities provide
We take for granted many of the services supplied by our local authorities. Find out how many services your local authority provides. Try to get the information from your library or local council offices, or ask your tutor for help.

Present your findings as a poster display. You may also wish to explain this poster to other people in your group.

For help with your research, see the Toolkit on page 4.

Investigating working in business

Business departments – where things get done

'3rd floor: Administration and Marketing'

'2nd floor: Production and Personnel'

'1st floor: Finance'

Unless you are the only person in a business, the work is normally divided into different areas or **departments**. In this way, a business hopes to be efficient in how it manages its staff, time and money.

Departments in companies are like those in a store such as Debenhams plc:

- the bigger the store, the more departments there are; each selling a different item
- the bigger the company, the more departments there will be; each performing a different job for the business.

Different types of businesses are organised into different departments, depending on:

- the size of the company
- what the company produces, sells or provides
- how the management or owners decide to use specific people for specific jobs.

For this element, you need to know about the following departments:

Distribution | Administration | Human Resources | Production | Marketing | Purchasing | Finance | Research and Development

Each department in a company exists for a reason – each has a purpose within the company. Look at the example of A.S. Paper Products plc.

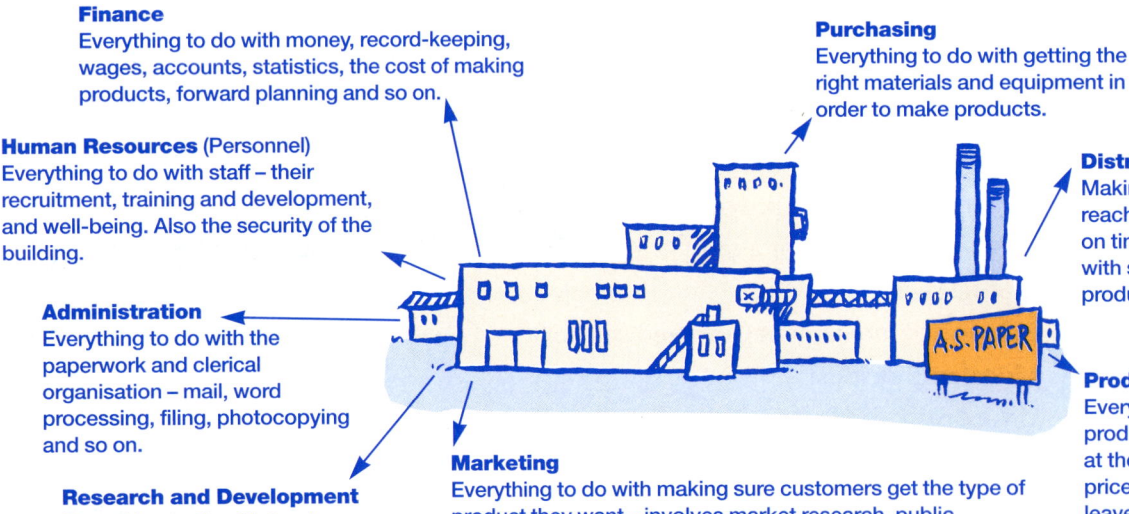

Finance
Everything to do with money, record-keeping, wages, accounts, statistics, the cost of making products, forward planning and so on.

Human Resources (Personnel)
Everything to do with staff – their recruitment, training and development, and well-being. Also the security of the building.

Administration
Everything to do with the paperwork and clerical organisation – mail, word processing, filing, photocopying and so on.

Research and Development
Everything to do with turning new or improved ideas into products or services to keep up with competitors.

Purchasing
Everything to do with getting the right materials and equipment in order to make products.

Distribution
Making sure the product reaches customers safely and on time. It is also concerned with storing materials and products.

Production
Everything to do with producing the right products, at the right time, for the right price. Before the products leave the production area, they have to be checked to ensure their quality is right.

Marketing
Everything to do with making sure customers get the type of product they want – involves market research, public relations and customer care.

Activity
The right task in the right department
Prepare a display showing which of the departments shown above is responsible for each of the following tasks: staff interviews; computer services; sales promotions; salaries; research into new products; packaging goods; transportation; leisure facilities for staff; overtime payments; reception; obtaining loans.

For ideas on how to use images in your display see the Toolkit on page 14.

Business organisations and personnel in departments

Job titles and their responsibilities – who does what?

A job title is the term used to describe what someone does within an organisation. Large companies have many different job titles and many people performing jobs. These people will be linked to job grades, ranks or positions.

People in different levels and types of jobs have different tasks and duties to carry out in order to make sure that jobs are done well. Their tasks may increase in number and difficulty according to the importance of the job – the more senior the job; the more duties, tasks, decisions, and responsibilities there will be.

Managing Director

In a large company the Managing Director holds the most important position. He or she is in overall charge of the company; is appointed by the board of directors; and leads the company in the right direction for both shareholders and employees.

Department Managers

Department Managers are responsible to the Managing Director and other directors. In a large company, each Department Manager is in charge of all the staff and the day-to-day running of a department. They make important decisions about their departments and must be able to manage people.

Other Workers

The other staff are responsible to the managers. They have a wide range of skills, qualifications and experience so they can do their jobs well. A successful company has staff who can work together as a team.

Can you make it to the top?

What are people in charge of?

'I am a Marketing Manager and I am in charge of managing the Marketing and Sales department of the company for which I work. I make sure that the right products reach the right customers and that they keep buying them.

I am responsible for all aspects of market research, customer service, sales and advertising.

I am responsible for some staff; for example, the customer service staff who serve people.'

Investigating working in business

'I am a Management Accountant and I am in charge of managing finance for the company for which I work.

I manage the incoming and outgoing money belonging to the company. I am also in charge of the staff who work in my department. These include wages clerks, who calculate workers' wages.'

'I am a Production Manager and I am in charge of managing production for the company for which I work.

This means I am responsible for everything to do with the ordering of materials, the production of goods and the control of their quality.

I am also in charge of the production workers who produce the goods.'

'I am a Managing Director of the company for which I work. I was appointed by the **board of directors**.

I have overall responsibility for the way the company is run. I lead the company and say what its purpose should be – what it aims to do. I hope to make it a successful company.

I am responsible for making sure the company is legally and correctly run. I give advice about the company to the shareholders.'

'I am a Department Manager and I am in charge of managing the Human Resources department for the company for which I work. This means I am responsible for everything to do with staff.

I am responsible for managing the recruitment, training and welfare of staff. I work with trade unions and make sure that all regulations to do with conditions of work are met.

I am also in charge of security staff who provide security for the company. Some people call me the Human Resource Manager.'

'We are administration staff and we help most of the departments in the company for which we work.

We are responsible for handling different types of paperwork, documentation, filing and word processing for the company.'

Business organisations and personnel in departments

Activity
Jobs and responsibilities

1 Now that you know something about job titles and responsibilities, can you place the following job titles in an organisational chart?

Managing Director, Marketing Manager, Management Accountant, Production Manager, Human Resource Manager, customer service staff, wages clerks, security staff, administration staff

Copy the chart below – the most senior title has already been filled in for you. Remember to work from the most senior downwards, and to place the jobs in the correct departments.

2 Interview at least two people in employment to find out what their jobs involve. These interviews could be with people you met on your work experience or people you work with in a part-time job. Ask them:
- What is your job title?
- What tasks do you carry out?
- What decisions do you have to make, if any?
- What are your main responsibilities?

You can present your findings as a short talk or as a chart, showing the main results of your interviews.

MANAGING DIRECTOR

Assignment

Chamber of Commerce competition

Setting the scene

Your local Chamber of Commerce is running a competition for students following GNVQ Foundation Business programmes. The organisers hope the competition will encourage students to find out as much as they can about the different types of business organisations and the people who work in them. You have decided to enter.

Your tutor gives you the following information.

Task 1
To show your knowledge of the different types of business organisation, write a list of different business organisations, with examples.

Task 2
Decide which businesses to use for your study.

It might be helpful to contact businesses where you know someone – perhaps through work experience, a part-time job, previous assignments, family contacts, or friends.

Arrange by telephone or letter to interview someone at each business in order to find out the information listed in Task 3. Write down the names of the businesses and how you came to choose them. Keep a record of your phone conversation and/or interview with the businesses. You need the information about three businesses for your portfolio of evidence.

For more on writing business letters and telephoning, see the Toolkit on pages 9 and 12.

WIN COMPUTER EQUIPMENT *for your* **School or College!**

Make a study of the different types of businesses in your area. Find out about jobs in those businesses and the people who carry out those jobs. Present your findings on paper, video, audio tape, with photographs and so on.

SEE YOUR TUTOR FOR DETAILS

Task 3
Find out the following information about each organisation:
a the purpose, type, size and features of the business
b its main activities, with examples of products, goods and services provided and sold
c details of where the business is located (include maps and directions).

Make notes of, or record, any interviews.

Task 4
Choose any two departments from any of the businesses. Prepare an organisational chart for each department, showing the structure of the department including lines of responsibility.

Task 5
Interview three people who do different jobs in each of the two departments (six people in total). Find out their job titles, and what tasks and responsibilities go with their jobs. You may wish to video or tape record these interviews – with their permission.

Task 6
Assemble all the information you have collected for Tasks 1 to 4. Present your findings using any combination of the following: on paper with written notes, charts, maps, on video or audio tape, with photographs of the businesses and people.

Opportunities to collect evidence

In this assignment you should cover:

Element 3.1
PC1
PC2
PC3
PC4

Application of Number
Element 1.2

Communication
Element 1.1
Element 1.2
Element 1.3
Element 1.4

Information Technology
Element 1.3

Investigating working in business

❓ Quiz

How much do you know about business organisations?

1 If you run a business on your own, you are:
   a a partner
   b a sole trader
   c a local authority
   d a private company

2 If you can sell shares to your family and friends and your company is called P.B. Stone Ltd. you are:
   a a private limited company
   b a public limited company
   c a franchise
   d a partnership

3 Mr Ghoneim, Mrs Cook, Mr Gainda and Miss Carter are dentists who work together. They are:
   a sole traders
   b partners
   c part of a private limited company
   d part of a public limited company

4 If you have the letters **plc** after your company name, you are:
   a a private limited company
   b a local authority
   c a public limited company
   d personally responsible for all debts

5 If you are part of a franchise you get to keep:
   a all of the profits
   b most of the profits
   c none of the profits
   d all of the sales income

6 If you are in the personnel department you deal with:
   a quality control
   b financial matters
   c advertising campaigns
   d training staff

7 If you are in the administration department you deal with:
   a handling mail
   b vehicle repairs
   c security
   d financial matters

8 If you are a Managing Director you are responsible for:
   a working out wages
   b controlling marketing plans
   c running the company
   d production control

9 If you are responsible for quality control of goods you are:
   a a customer service assistant
   b a security officer
   c a production manager
   d the financial accountant

10 Can you spot the following words to do with job titles? Watch out! They might go back to front or diagonally.

Marketing Manager	Personnel Manager	Managing Director
Clerical staff	Service	Management
Security	Production Manager	Accountant
Wages clerks	Customer	Workers

P	R	O	D	U	C	T	I	O	N	M	A	N	A	G	E	R	Q
E	K	N	I	R	E	M	O	T	S	U	C	J	K	Y	O	E	C
R	V	C	S	W	E	Y	U	K	L	O	I	M	A	T	N	M	I
S	E	R	V	I	C	E	H	S	D	N	I	G	C	L	I	Z	X
O	G	Y	C	R	K	O	F	B	A	W	Y	E	C	M	O	P	N
N	M	S	V	Y	H	A	I	U	N	L	R	J	O	B	S	H	Y
N	H	R	A	O	M	B	C	N	A	I	U	I	U	X	K	Y	E
E	V	E	R	T	F	E	M	C	D	A	W	N	N	I	R	J	P
L	I	K	P	I	U	F	A	G	E	S	C	O	T	U	E	R	C
M	A	R	G	J	Y	M	N	I	K	H	B	F	A	U	L	B	T
A	N	O	K	N	D	I	A	D	S	E	F	E	N	V	C	E	O
N	O	W	F	R	G	C	G	R	I	D	E	N	T	C	S	L	T
A	V	X	S	A	C	F	E	L	Y	T	I	R	U	C	E	S	N
G	E	R	N	V	Y	H	M	D	A	N	M	A	N	E	G	E	S
E	S	A	P	O	C	L	E	R	I	C	A	L	S	T	A	F	F
R	M	R	W	E	C	H	N	C	T	G	T	A	S	E	W	G	V
U	K	L	B	Y	F	V	T	B	N	A	D	E	R	D	V	A	O
S	M	A	R	K	E	T	I	N	G	M	A	N	A	G	E	R	T

Scoring

If you scored:

- between 1 and 4 – you need to go back and re-read this section or redo the quiz.
- between 5 and 7 – you have a sound understanding of business organisations.
- 8 or more – you have done very well and have an excellent knowledge of business organisations.

See page 134 for the answers.

Investigate jobs in business

What shall I do? *Manager?* *Accountant?*
Computer programmer? *Salesperson?*

In the last element we looked at different types of business organisations, the departments within them and the jobs done by people who work there. This element builds on what you discovered in the last element as you begin to investigate in more detail the types of jobs in business which might be suitable as future employment for you.

This is a valuable element, as it gives you an opportunity to investigate jobs which really interest you. It may even help you decide what to do when you finish your studies.

By the end of this element you should be able to:
- seek advice and information from appropriate sources when necessary
- identify two jobs in business which are likely to suit you
- describe the main purposes of each identified job
- explain why each identified job is likely to suit you
- identify the main skills required for each identified job
- identify qualifications required for each identified job
- identify how to obtain the skills and qualifications required for each identified job.

Help! I need some advice

Throughout your working life – from the day you start your first job until the day you retire – you can always get help and advice about your job, and everything to do with it. This might be help about training, promotion, re-training courses and so on. The information and advice is always there, but you have to know where to go in order to get the right advice at the right time.

For those of you about to begin full-time employment, probably the most important source of advice and information will be your careers adviser. S/he will give you as much help as you need about courses and jobs, including advice and information on:
- the purposes of jobs
- the suitability of jobs for you
- the likelihood of jobs being available to you.

For more on careers advisers, see page 124.

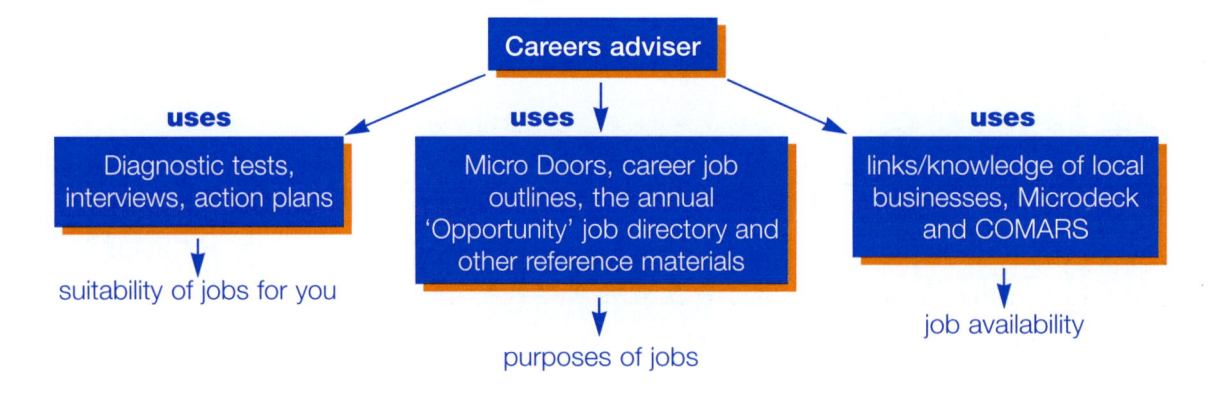

Investigating working in business

```
                    Careers adviser
         uses            uses              uses
    Diagnostic tests,  Micro Doors, career job   links/knowledge of local
    interviews, action plans  outlines, the annual   businesses, Microdeck
                        'Opportunity' job directory and   and COMARS
                        other reference materials
         ↓                  ↓                    ↓
    suitability of jobs for you   purposes of jobs    job availability
```

Other sources of information include:
- staff in your school or college, who will know lots of general information about employment areas
- people in industry and business who have links with your school or college. They might be involved in mock interviews, careers conventions, industry days
- staff in the personnel departments of businesses who can give help and advice on jobs and training
- reference materials found at careers and lending libraries; for example, *Jobfinder* magazine
- various training organisations which offer YTS or TEC placements.

Activity
The role of your careers adviser

This might be a good time to invite your careers adviser to talk to your group about the range of help and information s/he can give you. Write down the main details of the talk.

What shall I do?

Most students begin to receive careers advice when they are in Year 9 of secondary school. Careers teachers and advisers help students think about the world of work and how they will one day be part of that world. You will continue to receive help and advice until you have found, and got, the right job for you.

'This is a triceratops'

'I'm studying geology and zoology next year'

'I'm curator at a national museum which specialises in fossils'

Sarah at 6

Sarah at 16

Sarah at 26

Every young person today knows that jobs aren't easy to find – enough people have told them so. That is why it's important you know as much as possible about the job opportunities open to you, and about yourself. Some people, like Sarah, are lucky enough to have a good idea of what they want to do in life from an early age. Her early childhood interest led to other hobbies and interests, both in and out of school and college, and eventually to a job which used her interests and talents.

> **Activity**
> **Interests and suitable jobs**
> What were your interests and favourite subjects when you were younger? Do you still have the same ones? You may need to ask your family to jog your memory. Write about your interests and word process your account.

Unfortunately, finding the right job isn't quite as easy for most of us. We may say, 'I've always been good with children', or 'I like meeting people and travelling', but that doesn't mean we all end up as nannies or coach drivers. If only finding the job which suits us were that easy.

When you begin to think about jobs, ask yourself these questions.

- How will I know when a job is right for me? (right conditions, tasks, responsibilities and so on)
- How will I know if I will be suitable for the job I would really like to do? (personality, skills, qualifications, interests)
- How likely is it that I will be able to do the job I most want to do? (jobs in your area, training, qualifications, age and so on)

How can you find the answers to these questions?

Getting help and advice

- Get as much **help and advice** as you can from people. Ask:
  - your careers adviser or teacher
  - family and friends who have jobs that interest you
  - people you know through part-time jobs, work experience, volunteer work.
- Gather as much **information** as you can about the jobs in which you are interested. Contact:
  - careers and guidance centres
  - libraries
  - local employers.
- Try to get some **experience** of the jobs you like – by work experience or at least by talking to people who have those jobs.

Getting to know yourself

- Get to **know yourself** as well as possible. Be honest and thoughtful when you ask yourself these sorts of questions.
  - What am I really interested in?
  - What am I good at?
  - What do I know? (skills and qualifications)
  - What are my weaknesses?
  - What would I hate to do?
  - What are my ambitions?
  - What are my plans for further study?

> **Activity**
> **Personal profile**
> Write a profile of yourself which answers all the questions above. Word process your profile.

Investigating working in business

What does it mean?

- **Diagnostic test** = a series of questions designed to get to know all about you and what job areas would suit you. It's a bit like answering a magazine quiz.

Some time during your GNVQ course you will probably have at least one interview with your local careers adviser. During your interview the adviser will ask you many questions in order to get an overall picture of you and how to help you get a suitable job. You might have to take a **diagnostic test**. All these things give your adviser as much information as possible about you as a future worker.

Suitable jobs – for now and later

Once you have an idea of the types of jobs in which you are interested and which might suit you, you need to investigate the jobs available to you, **now** and in **the future**.

Activity
A personal questionnaire

The following list of questions might help you decide exactly what your strengths are. Write down each question, and answer it as fully and honestly as possible. You could show your answers to the careers adviser or your tutor when you talk about your future plans.

All about you...

1. How important do you think work will be in your life?
2. How hard are you prepared to work in order to do well at your job/career?
3. How senior do you want to be in your job? (Do you have lots of ambition to do well?)
4. What sort of things give you most satisfaction:
   a at school or college?
   b at home?
5. What things do you think you are good at?
6. What qualifications are you likely to have at the end of your full-time education?
7. How prepared will you be to continue studying or training once you have a job?
8. How well will you cope with a job which has a definite routine – with each day being much the same as any other?
9. How far are you prepared to travel in order to do the job you want?
10. How much responsibility do you think you would like in a job?
11. How important is it for you to have a job which involves working with other people?
12. How important is it for your family to approve of the job you do?
13. How do you like to spend your spare time?
14. What skills do you think you will bring to your first job?

If your answers are vague and you have lots of 'don't knows' you should begin to think seriously about what you want from a job, and how an employer is likely to see you!

Finding the right job

If you look in the job section of your local newspaper you will see a variety of jobs, but many of them won't be suitable for a first job.

Activity
Suitable or unsuitable jobs?

Look at the following adverts. List why they might not be suitable for a first job.

•SOFTWARE ENGINEERS•
Home Counties, to £35,000
We are looking for two experienced engineers with skills including:
- UNIX
- DSP
- Network Management

The ideal candidates will have at least five years' experience of managing people and projects, and will be able to take a leading decision-making role in this progressive company.
Call Anthony Sharp on 01734 568394, or write quoting ref. 23/GH to Leading Lights Recruitment, 24 The Square, Uptown, Surrey GU2 5DL

DIVISIONAL SALES MANAGER

We are looking for a high flying individual with a degree in business administration and 10 years' experience of sales within the textiles industry. Must be a good strategist, with excellent communication skills and leadership qualities.

This is an excellent opportunity for the right person. Please apply enclosing curriculum vitae and contact number to:
Human Resource Manager, Redbridge Textiles, Crofton Place, London SW17 5DJ

MARKETING DIRECTOR

required for large City centre retail company. The ideal candidate will have excellent marketing qualifications, sound experience and understanding of the retail market, and proven people management skills. Must be willing to travel nationally (a company car will be provided).

Write in confidence, with a detailed CV, to the Chief Executive, Rathbone Retail, Cuthbert Street, Bristol BS1 4UD

A visit to your local careers centre or Job Centre might also provide information about different types of jobs.

Investigate jobs in business

What to look for?

A first job
- Do you have the right qualifications and skills if they are asked for?
- Is training given?
- Can you continue to study on day release?
- Can you get to it reasonably easily?
- Does it seem an interesting job?

A job for someone with more experience
- Can you continue to train for further progression?
- Is your experience in other jobs useful?
- Does the salary give credit for qualifications and experience?
- Will you be given more responsibility?

What are employers looking for?

In the last element we found out that a company's Human Resource (or Personnel) department is responsible for recruiting staff. Once a vacancy occurs, the Human Resource Manager, or an assistant, will place advertisements for the job and will write a job description and specification with the help of the department which has the vacancy.

A **job advertisement** outlines:
- the job title
- qualifications and skills needed
- experience needed
- salary/wage offered
- hours
- how and where to apply.

A **job description** or **specification** details:
- the purpose of the jobs – **tasks** and **responsibilities**
- personal qualities looked for
- qualifications and skills needed
- training and courses provided
- working conditions
- holidays.

For example, the job description and specification for the post of **clerical assistant** shown above might look something like this.

Activity
A suitable job
What makes this a suitable first job? Give as many reasons as possible, looking at the range under suitability.

Clerical Assistant

Young person required with good general education and some knowledge of computers. Lively personality - must be willing to learn as training will be given.

FOR MORE INFORMATION OR AN APPLICATION FORM, CONTACT: PERSONNEL OFFICER • JG BALLARDS LTD. ENGINEERS • 62 MACRAE STREET • WESTGATE • LEICESTERSHIRE • 01756 389574

Job Vacancy (Description)
Job – Clerical assistant in company's administration department. JG Ballards Ltd. is a small light engineering company making parts for the motor trade.
Tasks – Assisting with record-keeping and filing, some word processing; some telephone work.
Hours – 8.30–4.30; Mon – Sat

Job Vacancy (Specification)
Qualifications – Good general education; knowledge of Word Perfect; Typing RSA II.
Qualities – Must work well as part of a team; lively and enthusiastic.
Skills – Good numeracy and communication skills; good telephone manner; polite and friendly.

What do they mean?

- **Job description = what you can expect from a job, including tasks and responsibilities.**
- **Job specification = what is expected of the person who will carry out the job; the type of person needed, their skills, qualifications and so on.**

Investigating working in business

What do they mean?

- **Tasks** = activities you will be expected to carry out in order to do your job.
- **Responsibilities** = being relied on to carry out the tasks correctly and to the best of your ability.

Activity
Tasks and responsibilities

1. List all the tasks and all the responsibilities you have at home and at school/college. Can you put them in order of importance?
2. Interview one or two friends or members of your family to find out the main tasks and responsibilities of their jobs. Write them down.
3. Look at the 'Situations Vacant' section of your local newspaper. Select three advertisements for jobs and for each job complete a chart like the one shown below.

Job one: _____
Job description: _____

Job specification: _____

The opportunities available
- are there job openings in your area?
- have you seen the job advertised?
- what types of jobs are available in your area?

Your circumstances
- can you get to it reasonably easily?
- can you get to it on time?
- can you afford to travel to it?

→ **A job for you** ←

↓

Your interests
- do you like doing what the job would ask of you?
- does it match your skills and qualifications?
- would you feel happy doing the job – all the tasks and responsibilities?

Suitable jobs for suitable people

As part of the evidence for your portfolio for this element, you must select two jobs which are likely to be suitable for you. For both jobs – one as a possibility for first employment and the second intended for further progression – you must say why they would be suitable for you. To help decide whether or not a job is suitable, you should consider the following things:

- your circumstances
- your interests
- the opportunities available.

Activity
Which job for Tom?

'I don't like too much routine but I'm patient'

'I'm learning to drive, but I won't be able to buy my own car for ages'

'I like meeting people. I wouldn't like to work on my own'

Tom has recently completed his Foundation Business GNVQ, and is now looking for a first job in some sort of business administration. He has had two work experience placements in offices, has taken part in young enterprise as the team's accountant, and has a part-time job in a local DIY store.

He has three GCSEs; in English, maths and geography. He is interested in computers and rowing. He enjoys working as part of a team.

He is learning to drive. He lives four miles from the centre of town, on a bus route.

Study the following three job advertisements. Decide which you think would best suit Tom. Be sure to take into account the three points of opportunity, interest and circumstance when you make your choice.

When you have decided, write a report on Tom as his careers officer, advising him which job you think he should take, and why.

TRAVEL AGENCY ASSISTANT
Required to work in CITY CENTRE TRAVEL AGENCY. Must have knowledge of computers and good general education. Opportunity for day-release to study NVQ Administration

CLERICAL ASSISTANT on Business Park
To work in general office and assist Office Manager. Would suit someone with previous experience of record keeping, invoicing and basic stock control. Level II Business qualification essential

SALES REP
To cover the south-west for multi-national company – no cold selling, but knowledge of security sysyems desirable. Must be hard-working and a car-driver.

Investigate jobs in business

Skills for jobs

Assistant, trainee, apprentice, junior, learner – all desirable people who have not yet learnt the skills of the job they hope to do well. To be skilled at your job means you can do a series of, often complicated, tasks without help or supervision and in a competent and professional way. Skills are acquired through experience, training and practice.

When you first begin work you won't be expected to have all the skills to do the job. These are called **vocational** or job skills. Some jobs need more vocational skills than others:

- a chef in charge of a restaurant kitchen will have many more skills than the assistant who prepares the vegetables
- a personal secretary to a company director will have many more skills than the assistant who does the photocopying.

Secretary: using the computer, telephone and fax machine; filing, record-keeping

Chef: weighing, baking, roasting, grilling; making up recipes

Some skills are common to most jobs. For example, both the chef and the personal secretary will speak on the telephone to people, learn to give directions to others, and will be organised and thorough. These types of skills are called **core skills**. They are important as you can take them with you as you progress in your career. They are sometimes called **transferable skills** as you can transfer them from one job to another. Examples of core skills are:

- being flexible and able to learn new ways of doing things
- being able to work as a member of a team, fitting in with other workers and dealing with customers
- being competent and careful with tasks to be completed.

Core skills can be learnt at school and college, along with some vocational skills such as word processing. The pattern of your working life is likely to look like this to begin with:

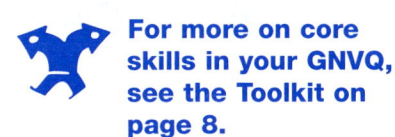

> For more on core skills in your GNVQ, see the Toolkit on page 8.

Basic Vocational Skills + Core Skills = 1st Job + Training + Practice = More Vocational + Skills

More Core Skills + Training + Practice = 2nd Job + Training....and so on...

Investigating working in business

Activity
Skills for jobs

Look at the first two lists below – one of jobs; and one of skills. Try to match the jobs to the skills.

Jobs:
- junior clerk, accountant, secretary, receptionist, shop assistant, mechanic, hairdresser

Skills:
- good with numbers, good with hands, gets on well with other people, very well organised, responsible, always polite, very careful

Which of the following do you consider to be useful core skills?

Core skills:
- good eyesight, keyboard skills, a friendly manner, physical strength, liking animals, punctuality, good at figures, design flair, able to cook, good at problem-solving, map-reading, able to use a computer, good at organising different things, able to take orders, enjoy working in a group

Qualifications for jobs

Some people leave school without any qualifications, and there are jobs available which don't ask for any. However, most employers will want to know which exam courses you studied and what your grades were. Generally speaking, the more qualifications you have the greater your choice when it comes to selecting a job.

You have decided to study for a GNVQ – General National Vocational Qualification. You are hoping to gain a qualification which will help you get a job. As the name says, this course will give you a **vocational qualification**. You are studying at Foundation level.

At the end of the course you may either decide to find a job or to continue with your full-time studies, progressing to Intermediate and then possibly to Advanced GNVQs.

If you get a job, you might decide to continue studying part time to extend your knowledge and improve the skills needed to do your job well. In this case, you may study for an NVQ – National Vocational Qualification.

You can progress from level 1 through to level 5 as you gain more experience and knowledge. There are now NVQs offered in many job-related subjects; from administration and hairdressing to sheep-rearing... The list is endless. They help you progress in your job.

If you are studying for GCSEs as well as your GNVQ, you are hoping to gain an **academic qualification**. These are the qualifications normally offered at schools and colleges, and do not relate directly to jobs or the world of work.

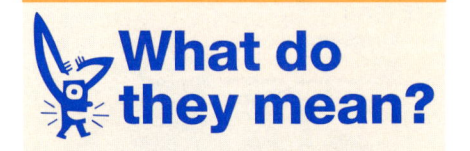

What do they mean?

- **Vocational qualifications** = related to jobs; help to increase knowledge of a work area; can be studied full time or as part of day release.

- **Academic qualifications** = not aimed at a specific job; usually studied full time at school or college; involve learning the theory of a subject.

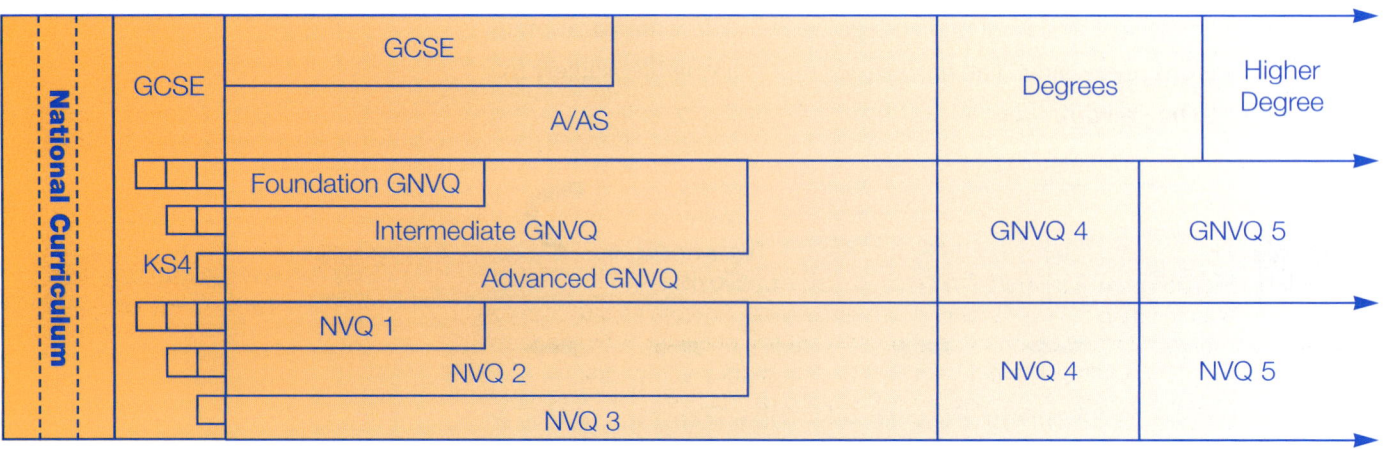

The pathways to academic and vocational qualifications

Investigate jobs in business

Activity
Vocational and academic qualifications

1. Talk to someone who has a job which interests you. Ask them what vocational and academic qualifications they had when they first started work. Find out if they have gained any more qualifications during their working life. If so, find out why they studied or trained for them; for example, was it to gain promotion?

2. Visit your careers library and/or guidance centre to look at computer programs such as Micro Doors; career job outlines; and 'Opportunity' materials, which have lots of information about jobs.

    Select two jobs which interest you. Find out what vocational and academic qualifications you need for them. (If you select one job suitable for first employment and one which needs more skills and experience, you can use this activity as preparation for your portfolio.)

How to get those qualifications

Nowadays it might be harder for you to find the right job, but it's much easier to get more qualifications and training. Not only is there a wider range of courses, but you can study for them in a wider range of places.

It is no longer just a case of staying on at sixth form or leaving, hoping to get on a training scheme. So it's worth thinking seriously about what qualifications you need and where you can get them.

'I've got a job in the office of an engineering firm and I'm studying for more GCSEs at night school'

'Which way do I go? They decided, now I've got to!'

'The local TEC arranged for me to work and train at a local estate agent's. I love it and hope to sell houses one day'

'School wasn't for me. I'm at Technical College studying for an NVQ in Administration.'

'I've got a full-time job in a local department store which does its own training'

'Well, I decided to stay on in full-time education. I'm at 6th form college taking an Intermediate Business GNVQ.'

'I'm working in a hotel as a receptionist and I'm studying through distance learning at home for my NVQ in Hotel Management'

'I've got a job as an office junior and I'm doing day-release at the local FE college, doing a CLAIT course.'

'I'm doing a YTS at the local council offices, learning about office routine and doing a day release to do a City and Guilds'

Decide on your job, and then make sure you have or can get the right qualifications

Activity
Finding out about further qualifications

With the help of your tutor and careers adviser, find out as much as you can about the opportunities on offer at any two of the places mentioned in the picture above. For example, what courses do your local sixth form and further education colleges offer? What are the main types of suitable YTS placements provided in your area?

For help with your research, see the Toolkit on page 4.

Investigating working in business

Assignment

Newspaper article

Setting the scene

The 'Business World' section of your local paper is publishing a series of articles on business opportunities for young people. It has invited students of business to write articles about jobs which interest them or which they might wish to do once they have finished studying.

You have decided to write an article. Your tutor advises you to write about a career which interests you; beginning with a first-time job which might lead to promotion or progression once you have gained more skills and qualifications.

Task 1
Select the career you intend to research for your article. You may want to look again at the job titles and departments on page 109 to help you decide. You may also want to check the careers library for information.

Task 2
Decide which job you think would be suitable for a first-time job in your chosen career. Explain why this job would suit you.

Task 3
For this job, make notes on the following:
  a the purpose of the job
  b skills and qualifications needed
  c how to obtain these skills and qualifications.

Task 4
Find out about a job which would be a likely progression from this first job. It should be a job which would be interesting and suitable for you. Explain why the job would suit you.

Task 5
For this job, make notes on the following:
  a the purpose of the job
  b skills and qualifications needed
  c how to obtain these skills and qualifications.

Task 6
Use your notes from Tasks 3 and 5 to write the newspaper article. Include a headline and any other headings, photographs and so on.

Word process your article using column layout to make it look realistic.

Opportunities to collect evidence

In this assignment you should cover:

Element 3.2
- PC1
- PC2
- PC3
- PC4
- PC5
- PC6
- PC7

Communication
- Element 1.1
- Element 1.2
- Element 1.4

Information Technology
- Element 1.1
- Element 1.2
- Element 1.3
- Element 1.4

Investigate jobs in business

?Quiz

How much do you know about investigating jobs?

See page 134 for the answers.

1. Your local careers adviser can offer you advice on:
   a. national insurance
   b. full-time employment and courses
   c. hobbies and interests
   d. income tax

2. The careers library of your school or college will have:
   a. books on how to ski
   b. detailed information on one or two jobs
   c. general information on employment areas and courses
   d. modern novels

3. The Human Resource department of a business is a good place to seek help on getting a job in that business because:
   a. it controls the finances
   b. it helps with production
   c. it distributes goods
   d. it recruits and trains people

4. Which **one** of the following jobs would be suitable as a first job for a young person about to leave full-time education with three GCSEs in English, maths and computer studies:
   a. skilled mechanic
   b. office junior
   c. computer programmer
   d. personnel officer

5. Which **one** of the following jobs would be suitable for further progression for someone with five years' experience in a company's Finance department:
   a. clerical assistant
   b. production manager
   c. company director
   d. assistant manager of an accounts department

6. Which **one** of the following is **not** a qualification needed for a job in an office:
   a. GCSE English
   b. Foundation GNVQ Business
   c. ability to work on your own
   d. RSA II typing

7. Which **one** of the following would **not** be considered a **core skill** for someone about to train as a production worker in a factory:
   a. good at practical work
   b. ability to work as part of a team
   c. Intermediate GNVQ Manufacturing
   d. good with numbers

8. Which course would be suitable for someone wishing to obtain further qualifications in business administration who already has NVQ Level II in Administration:
   a. GCSE Business Studies
   b. City & Guilds Numberpower
   c. Intermediate GNVQ Business
   d. NVQ Level III in Administration

Scoring

If you scored:
- between 1 and 3 – you perhaps aren't too sure what skills and qualifications are needed for jobs. Ask your tutor for advice!
- between 4 and 6 – your understanding of skills and where to get advice is reasonable. What weren't you sure about?
- 7 and above – your understanding of this element is very good. You should know exactly where to go to get help about a suitable job for yourself.

Investigating working in business

Plan for employment in business

In the last element we looked at the types of jobs available in the world of business and the organisations in which these jobs can be found. In this element you will begin to plan how to go about getting one of these jobs – perhaps the job you investigated as suitable for your first job.

There may be quite a number of people chasing the same job as you, so it is important you know where to get the right advice and what you need to do to get a job.

By the end of this element you should be able to:
- seek advice and information from appropriate sources when necessary
- identify personal information and produce a curriculum vitae (CV)
- describe the main ways to find out about job vacancies in business
- describe the main stages in recruitment in business
- describe different ways of presenting personal information to prospective employers.

Help!

Applying for jobs can seem difficult when you first start. But remember, there are many people who will offer you help and advice about each stage in getting a worthwhile and interesting job.

Careers advisers:
- will give help and advice about jobs, training courses, higher education and so on. They organise careers conventions and mock interviews. They are specially trained to guide you towards the right course or job. They help you assess your personal skills.

Careers staff in schools and colleges:
- have been on courses to learn how to help students find jobs and courses. They work with the careers guidance advisers. They can arrange interviews with careers advisers.

For more on careers advisers, see page 113.

Personal information – giving the right details

When you apply for a job it is very important you know what details you should supply to the person who is in charge of recruiting staff (this might be an owner, a manager or someone in charge of personnel). Whoever it is, s/he will be the first person to read all about you and decide how suitable you might be for the job you want. It is sometimes worth finding out the name of the person in charge of recruiting, so you can write to them by name.

Plan for employment in business

Employers recently told the Careers Advisory Service that as many as 75% of all people applying for jobs get turned down almost as soon as their applications are read because they do **not** show they are able to do the job. This does not mean that they are all unsuitable, but it does mean most do not supply the correct information.

When you have found a job for which you want to apply, look carefully at the **job description** and **specification** so that your application shows an employer that you have all the necessary **skills, personal qualities** and **qualifications**. If you do this well, you will probably get to the next stage – an interview.

So what types of information do you need to tell an employer, and how might you be asked to present these details?

A job which asks for a CV

Many of the jobs you see advertised will ask applicants to send a copy of their CV.

Below is an example of a job which does just that. You might think it is a suitable first-time job.

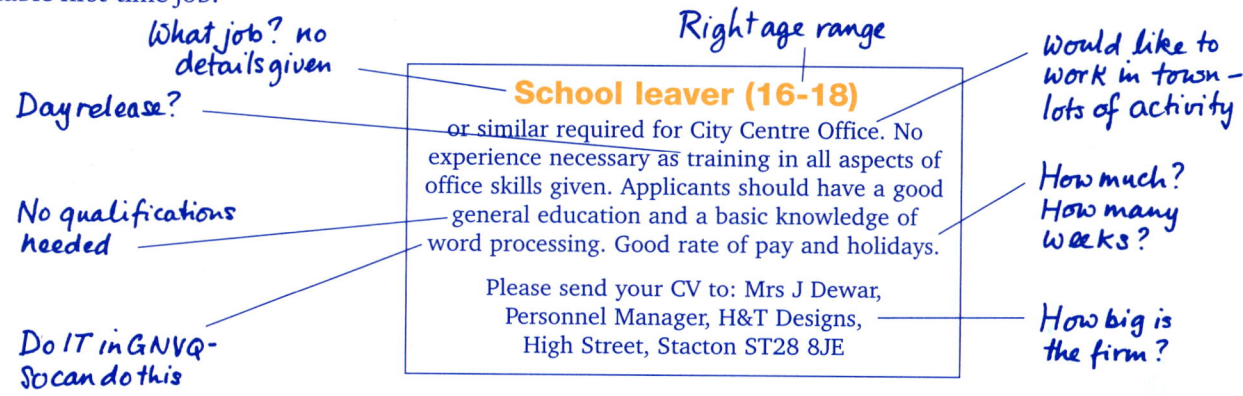

> **School leaver (16–18)**
> or similar required for City Centre Office. No experience necessary as training in all aspects of office skills given. Applicants should have a good general education and a basic knowledge of word processing. Good rate of pay and holidays.
>
> Please send your CV to: Mrs J Dewar, Personnel Manager, H&T Designs, High Street, Stacton ST28 8JE

Handwritten annotations:
- What job? no details given
- Day release?
- No qualifications needed
- Do IT in GNVQ – so can do this
- Right age range
- Would like to work in town – lots of activity
- How much? How many weeks?
- How big is the firm?

A CV for this, or any job, needs to include the following information:

- **Personal details** – name, address, telephone number, age
- **Education** – details of your college or school and the course(s) you are studying; for example, GCSEs, GNVQs, NVQs, City & Guilds, RSA, BTEC
- **Qualifications** – the subjects you have already gained at GCSE, GNVQ, NVQ, City & Guilds and so on
- **Training** – any youth training or vocational training you might have received. This will increase as you gain experience at work
- **Work experience** – any employment you have had, including part-time and holiday work and work experience
- **Interests** – any hobbies, sports, or activities such as scouting or volunteer work which you think might show what type of person you are. Don't list too many!
- **Additional information** – any skills or information you haven't been able to include elsewhere; for example, your ability to use a computer or having a driving licence
- **Referees** – the names, addresses and positions (for example, tutor, employer, headteacher) of two people who know you well. Always remember to ask if you can use their names.

For more about job descriptions and specifications, see page 117.

Activity
What employers look for

Using a job you investigated in the last element, list all the things you think the employer is looking for. Keep this for later use.

What does it mean?

- CV = the initials for a Latin phrase, 'curriculum vitae'. It simply means a record or list of what you have done in your life so far. It is an outline of your achievements.

Investigating working in business

Activity
All about you

On a piece of paper write down the following:
- every skill you think you have
- everything you think you're good at
- all your qualifications – already taken and being studied for
- your interests – in and out of school or college
- any part-time jobs and work experience placements you've had
- any responsibilities given to you either at work or school or college.

These details will help you complete a personal CV and a letter of application.

Remember: Skills could include things such as:
- getting on with people
- being able to work without much help
- being good at speaking to people
- being able to work as part of a team.

Your CV will look good if it is...
- word processed (it is also easier to change it if you keep it on disc)
- well presented, attractive and easy to read
- to the point – it is a list of your achievements, not a letter, and should never be more than two sides long
- easy to follow, with information in the right order – put your latest courses, jobs and qualifications first.

Here is the CV of a student who has decided to apply for the job advertised on page 125.

CURRICULUM VITAE

NAME: Benjamin Jones **DATE OF BIRTH:** 13.05.77

ADDRESS: 7 Carters Road **TELEPHONE:** 01731 56301
Stacton
ST24 4HT

EDUCATION:
1994-present: West Bay College, Stacton
1990-1994:   Testville School, Stacton

QUALIFICATIONS:
AWAITED:
I am at present studying for my Business Foundation GNVQ which includes Communication, Numeracy and Information Technology. I am also hoping to improve my grade in GCSE English. I am taking GCSE geography for the first time.

ACHIEVED:
GCSEs: English Language   (F)   Computer Studies (E)
Science   (E)
Maths   (D)

WORK EXPERIENCE:
I have completed two work experience placements, each for two weeks:
1994 - office work in Ford car dealers
1993 - sales assistant in a sportswear shop
I also have a part-time job in a local hotel, The Vine at Stacton.
I help at the reception desk and in the restaurant.

INTERESTS:
I am a keen football player and I am a member of the college 2nd XI team. I also enjoy playing table tennis. I am a Scout and help with a local cub pack.

ADDITIONAL INFORMATION:
I have a certificate in First Aid.
I am learning to drive.

REFERENCES:
Mrs S Smithson (Headteacher)   Mr C Prowting (Scout Leader)
Testville School   18 Harrow Lane
Stacton   Stacton
ST25 6HR   ST23 8TH

Some people put their personal information, including name, address, date of birth and telephone number, at the end of their CV.

You will write your own CV as part of your work for this element.

Plan for employment in business

Ways to find out about jobs

The job advertisement on page 125 was taken from a local newspaper, but there are lots of other places to look for jobs...

Careers Office. Specially trained staff to advise you about further education, courses and jobs. Lots of information is kept on computer.

Job Centre. First-time jobs aren't usually displayed here. Jobs are displayed as self-service. Staff are trained to help. Most jobs are local.

Now where do I look?

Newspapers. Local newspapers are likely to have jobs for school/college leavers. Jobs go quickly – so don't delay!

Vacancy boards. Local firms often have boards with vacancies advertised. They will be in a place where lots of people can see them.

Local shops. Local shops often advertise jobs on their postcard display boards.

Employment agencies. These often specialise in office jobs, so are useful for finding jobs for clerical assistants, keyboard operators and so on. They don't charge you.

'We need an office junior in our office.'

'Do you have any vacancies?'

Friends and relatives. Who you know is important and can get you a job. Small firms often use word of mouth. Let people help you.

Direct approach. Don't wait for a job to be advertised. Phone or write to local firms. If they don't have details, they might keep you in mind when they do. You could consider writing to the business where you had your work experience. They know what you are capable of and may consider your application.

Investigating working in business

Activity
Finding out about job vacancies

Below are some ideas for activities to help you understand how different organisations advertise jobs and recruit people. The activities could be divided between the members of your group. If you divide up these activities, keep a record of who does each task.

- Visit your local Job Centre. Find out what types of jobs are usually displayed there. How suitable are they for young people? Collect any leaflets which might have useful information about jobs and/or training.
- Look in your local telephone directory or **Yellow Pages** to find the addresses of any employment agencies in your area. Find out, by visiting or telephoning them, what types of jobs they specialise in and for whom they find jobs. Write one or two paragraphs on your findings.
- Look in your local newspaper for examples of job advertisements. How many of them are suitable for young people? What types of jobs are they? Cut them out and stick them on a piece of paper.
- Arrange to visit a firm such as your local supermarket or DIY superstore to investigate how they recruit people. Do they have a vacancy board? What jobs are currently advertised there? Write down the details.
- Invite your local careers adviser to talk to your group about how the Guidance and Careers Centre helps young people get jobs and training. Record the talk.
- Ask two people you know how they found out about their jobs, and what they had to do to get them.

Activity
Ways of recruiting

Approach a business in your area and find out what stages they use when they are recruiting staff. Do different jobs need different ways of recruiting?

How do their methods match the five-point plan shown here?

Draw up your own plan for recruitment. Compare it with the one used by the business you investigated.

You have found the job, now what happens?

You've found a job which you would like to do. So, what are the main stages you can hope to go through before getting the job you want?

The five-point plan of recruitment

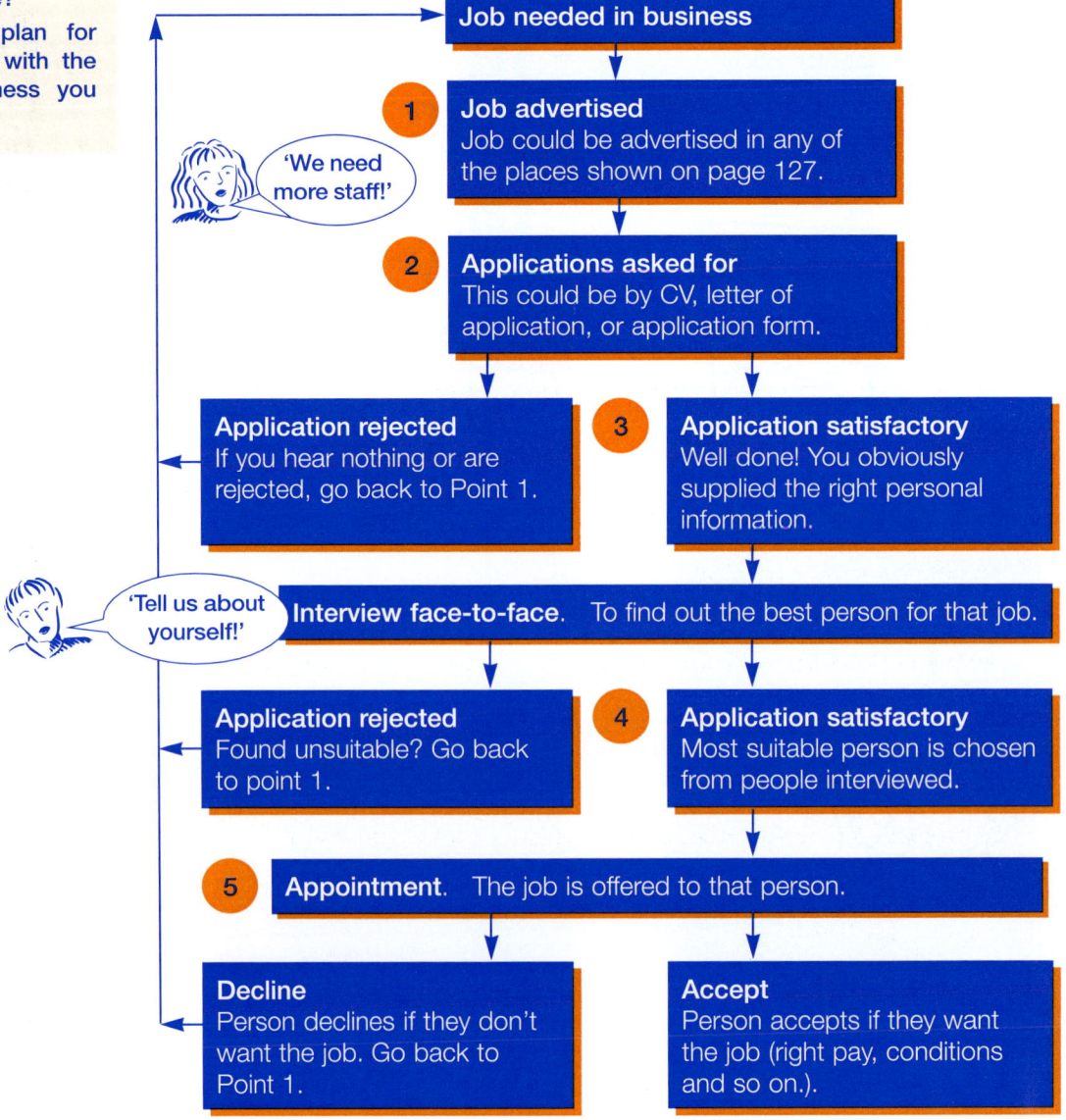

Job needed in business

'We need more staff!'

1 Job advertised
Job could be advertised in any of the places shown on page 127.

2 Applications asked for
This could be by CV, letter of application, or application form.

Application rejected
If you hear nothing or are rejected, go back to Point 1.

3 Application satisfactory
Well done! You obviously supplied the right personal information.

'Tell us about yourself!'

Interview face-to-face. To find out the best person for that job.

Application rejected
Found unsuitable? Go back to point 1.

4 Application satisfactory
Most suitable person is chosen from people interviewed.

5 Appointment. The job is offered to that person.

Decline
Person declines if they don't want the job. Go back to Point 1.

Accept
Person accepts if they want the job (right pay, conditions and so on.).

Plan for employment in business

How else might I have to apply for a job?

Not all jobs ask for a CV. Look at the job advertisement on the right, also from a local newspaper. Notice that this asks young people to apply in writing.

Letters of application

Job advertisements which ask you to apply in writing want you to write a **letter of application**. In this type of letter you should include details about yourself and why you are suitable for the job. You might also attach a copy of your CV, as this gives more information about your qualifications and experience. Your Record of Achievement will also tell the employer a lot.

A student decided to apply for the job at Mills Printers. The letter she wrote might have looked something like this.

---

7 Grove Place
Presswell
PW24 BHT

Mrs Thomas
The Personnel Manager
Mills Printers Ltd.
Wide Lane
Presswell
PW24 4VT

14 May 1995

Dear Sir or Madam

I wish to apply for the job advertised in today's Evening Echo. I have enclosed a copy of my CV.

I am seventeen years old and a student at Lockwood College, studying for my Business Foundation GNVQ. I am also taking Computer Studies and Art and Design GCSEs.

I hope to leave college in the summer to work in an office, as I enjoy working with people as part of a team, and using computers. I have used both Apple Macintosh and IBM computers.

I have had two work experience placements in local offices and I have a part-time job in a local supermarket. In these jobs I have worked as part of a team as well as by myself.

My interests are swimming and helping with a 16-25 group for young people with special needs.

I am available for interview at any time. I look forward to hearing from you.
Yours faithfully

Simran Atwal

SIMRAN ATWAL

Young Person

Required for Clerical Department of a local printing works. No experience needed as training given in Clerical Finance and Computing work.
Apply in writing to the
**Personnel Department,
Mills Printers Ltd,
Wide Lane, Presswell
PW24 4VT**

A good letter of application should be:
- word processed if possible
- checked for correct spelling and punctuation
- written in paragraphs
- to the point, but saying something about:
  - what job you are applying for
  - what qualifications you have and how they relate to the job
  - why you are interested in the job, and why you would be good at it
  - all the information in the advertisement.

Activity
Writing a letter of application

Find out on which night your local paper contains the most job advertisements. With help, select a job which seems interesting and suitable for you.

Write a letter of application for it.

If you can't find an advertisement, apply for the job advertised on page 12.

For more on writing formal letters, see the Toolkit on page 12.

Investigating working in business

Application forms

There is one last way in which you might be asked to supply information for a job. Often firms ask people to fill in **application forms** when they apply for a job. Firms use forms to help control the amount of paperwork they have to deal with.

An application form contains the same information as a CV or letter of application, but sometimes you may not have much space to write down all the information you think you should include. Also, you will only receive one copy of it to fill in. This means you must get it right by being prepared.

The checklist below will help you fill in an application form successfully.

Photocopy the form, or use separate sheets of paper, to practise writing answers	✓
Read the form carefully – at least twice	✓
Check any points/words not understood	✓
Check that all sections are answered	✓
Make sure your handwriting is neat, or use a computer if possible	✓
Check spellings and punctuation	
Keep information brief	
Use black ink	✓
Supply accurate information	
Keep a copy of the completed form	

For an application form you can photocopy and practise filling in, see the Toolkit on page 32.

Activity
Filling in application forms

- Photocopy the application form in the Toolkit section of this book (see page 32). Use it to practise filling in forms.
- As a group, see how many application forms you can collect. What information do they ask for?
- It is important to understand all that is asked of you on forms. Look at the following words and phrases which often appear on forms. Say what you think they mean. (The first has already been filled in, as an example.)

Word or phrase	Meaning
Surname	last name, family name
Marital status	
Nationality	
Details of any disability	
Chronological order	
Previous employment	
Relevant qualifications	
Status of referees	
Details of previous salary	
Canvassing will disqualify	
Posts of responsibility	

Plan for employment in business

Activity
What employers look for – an update
Look back at the list you made at the start of this section of the things you thought businesses were interested in when they employed someone. Update this list to include all the information you now know about recruitment.

> Look back at the Activity on page 125.

Assignment

The careers exhibition

Setting the scene
Your local Careers and Guidance Centre plans to hold a mini-careers exhibition, aimed at informing students about job opportunities in the area and what they need to do to get a job.

The careers advisers have asked Foundation GNVQ Business students to help stage this exhibition by providing information about how to plan for a job in business.

Task 1
Mount a display (A3-sized or larger) which shows the different ways to find out about job vacancies in your area. Include a collection of different vacancies from newspaper adverts, the Job Centre, shop notice-boards and so on. Video or take photographs of the display as part of your evidence.

Task 2
Use one of the vacancies which appeals to you as the basis for writing a simple CV and letter of application using your own details.

Use the CV and letter as examples for the exhibition – mount them as part of the display, or make them into a fact-sheet. Be sure to include hints on how to complete both a CV and a letter. Video or take photographs of this part of the exhibition.

Task 3
Produce a simple guide to completing application forms. Include a copy of an application form, using your own details as an example. There is one for you to photocopy in the Toolkit (see page 32).

Task 4
Arrange to interview someone who works in the personnel department of a local business organisation. Ask them what stages they must go through when they want to appoint someone to a vacancy.

Produce a chart which shows this information as clearly and simply as possible.

Task 5
Make a list of the most useful people to contact when seeking help about jobs and describe the types of information and help they might give. Use this as part of your display. You may wish to interview and record this advice.

> For more on interviewing people, see the Toolkit on page 8.

Opportunities to collect evidence
In this assignment you should cover:

Element 3.3	Information Technology	Communication
PC1	(if work is word processed)	Element 1.1
PC2	Element 1.1	Element 1.2
PC3	Element 1.2	Element 1.3
PC4	Element 1.3	Element 1.4
PC5		

Investigating working in business

❓ Quiz

What do you know about planning for jobs?

See page 134 for the answers.

1. Personal information is:
   a. any information stored on disk
   b. details about yourself – skills, interests and so on
   c. information made by personnel staff
   d. your opinions of work

2. Which one of the following is not a skill:
   a. working as a team
   b. Maths GCSE
   c. being able to ride a horse
   d. being able to speak French

3. A CV means:
   a. a current vacancy for a job
   b. the current value of the pound abroad
   c. a list of what you've done in life
   d. counting value for money

4. Careers advisers are trained to:
   a. test your reading skills
   b. help in the library
   c. write job advertisements
   d. help you find out about jobs

5. Local business jobs are advertised in:
   a. national newspapers
   b. local newspapers
   c. telephone books
   d. business directories

6. Job Centres are there to:
   a. advertise jobs in local businesses
   b. offer training for new jobs
   c. advertise all national jobs available
   d. write your CV

7. What is usually the next stage in recruitment after application?
   a. selection
   b. advertisement
   c. interview
   d. acceptance

8. At an interview, are you **most** likely to be asked:
   a. why you want the job
   b. how high you can jump
   c. what TV programmes you like
   d. to write an essay

Scoring

If you score:
- between 1 and 3 – you probably need to re-read this element, as your knowledge in this area is not too good.
- between 4 and 6 – you have a reasonable amount of knowledge about planning for jobs, but be sure to check any areas you may still be unsure about.
- 7 or 8 – you have a very good understanding of planning for jobs in business.

Useful addresses and organisations

The following organisations may be able to help you with information and advice. However, remember that they are busy, and don't overwhelm them with long lists of questions. Some may charge a small fee for carrying out research.

Banking Information Service
Lombard Street
London EC3V 9AT

British Safety Council
National Safety Centre
70 Chancellors Road
Hammersmith
London W6 9RS

Business in the Community
227a City Road
London EC1V 1LX

Council for Small Industries in Rural Areas (COSIRA)
141 Castle Street
Salisbury
Wilts

Crafts Council
44a Pentonville Road
London N1 9BY

Department of Employment
Caxton House
Tothill Street
London SW1H 9NF

The Princes Trust
8 Bedford Row
London WC1R 4BA

Skills and Enterprise Network
PO Box 12
West PDO
Leen Gate
Lenton
Nottingham NG7 2GB

You might also find it useful to contact local:
- employment offices
- branches of the Office of Fair Trading
- branches of the Health & Safety Executive.

Look for their details in your local telephone directory.

You may also find **The Employment Gazette** useful. Look for copies in the reference section of your public library.

Quiz answers

Unit 1 (page 65)

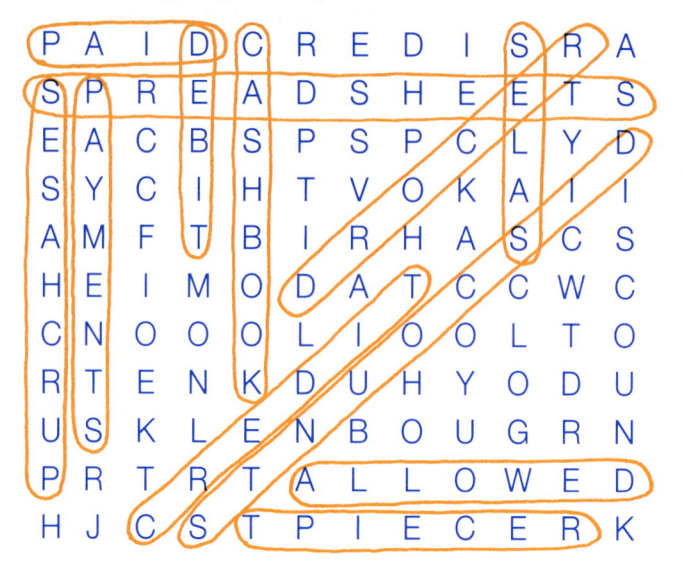

```
P A I D C R E D I S R A
S P R E A D S H E E T S
E A C B S P S P C L Y D
S Y C I H T V O K A I I
A M F T B I R H A S C S
H E I M O D A T C C W C
C N O O L I O O L T O
R T E N K D U H Y O D U
U S K L E N B O U G R N
P R T R T A L L O W E D
H J C S T P I E C E R K
```

1 – b, 2 – c, 3 – a, 4 – d, 5 – a, 6 – b, 7 – a, 8 – d, 9 – c, 10 – a, 11 – a, 12 – b

Element 2.1 (page 78)

1 – b, 2 – b, 3 – c, 4 – c, 5 – c, 6 – d, 7 – b, 8 – a, 9 – b, 10 – c, 11 – c, 12 – b

Element 2.2 (page 88)

1 – c, 2 – d, 3 – True, 4 – True, 5 – b, 6 – c, 7 – d, 8 – c, 9 – b, 10 – c

Element 2.3 (page 99)

1 – b, 2 – a, 3 – b, 4 – d, 5 – b, 6 – b, 7 – b

Element 3.1 (page 112)

1 – b, 2 – a, 3 – b, 4 – c, 5 – b, 6 – d, 7 – a, 8 – c, 9 – c

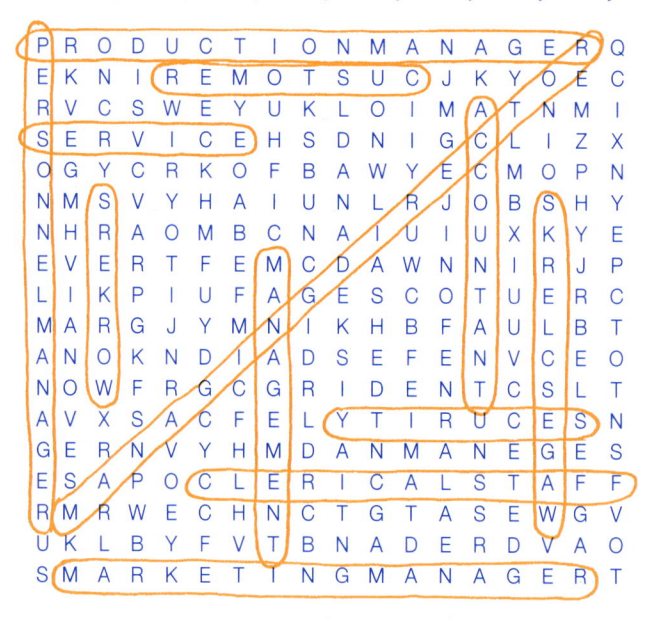

```
P R O D U C T I O N M A N A G E R Q
E K N I R E M O T S U C J K Y O E C
R V C S W E Y U K L O I M A T N M I
S E R V I C E H S D N I G C L I Z X
O G Y C R K O F B A W Y E C M O P N
N M S V Y H A I U N L R J O B S H Y
N H R A O M B C N A I U I U X K Y E
E V E R T F E M C D A W N N I R J P
L I K P I U F A G E S C O T U E R C
M A R G J Y M N I K H B F A U L B T
A N O K N D I A D S E F E N V C E O
N O W F R G C G R I D E N T C S L T
A V X S A C F E L Y T I R U C E S N
G E R N V Y H M D A N M A N E G E S
E S A P O C L E R I C A L S T A F F
R M R W E C H N C T G T A S E W G V
U K L B Y F V T B N A D E R D V A O
S M A R K E T I N G M A N A G E R T
```

Element 3.2 (page 123)

1 – b, 2 – c, 3 – d, 4 – b, 5 – d, 6 – c, 7 – c, 8 – d

Element 3.3 (page 132)

1 – b, 2 – b, 3 – c, 4 – d, 5 – b, 6 – a, 7 – a, 8 – a

Core skills coverage grid

Page	Activity/Assignment	Application of Number 1.1	1.2	1.3	Communication 1.1	1.2	1.3	1.4	Information Technology 1.1	1.2	1.3	1.4
17	Using percentages	*	*									
19	Reading graphs			*								
20	Using pictograms	*	*	*								
22	Using measurements	*	*	*								
25	Conversion graphs	*	*	*								
28	Using a spreadsheet	*	*	*					*	*	*	
30	Mean, mode and range		*									
36	Setting up a salon	*										
37	How do you pay for goods?	*	*	*	*		*		*		*	
39	Writing cheques	*				*						
40	Debit cards					*						
42	Spend, spend, spend	*	*	*		*						
44	Finding out about EPOS				*	*	*					
44	Getting to the bank					*						
47	Comparing receipts				*	*						
48	**Wright's Corner Shop**	*				*	*			*		
49	Invoice totals	*	*									
51	Completing invoices	*	*									
52	Spot the mistakes		*									
55	**Cristal's Health Club**		*						*		*	
56	Keeping track of your money		*									
58	Tally's tyres	*	*	*					*	*	*	
60	Filling in a cash book	*										
61	A cash book of your own	*	*	*		*			*	*		
62	Working out discounts	*	*						*	*		
64	**The Strange Sports Shop**	*				*					*	
68	Businesses around us	*				*						
70	Purposes of businesses	*				*	*					
72	Logos, signs and names						*					
73	Goods and services you use	*				*						
73	What do you know?					*	*					
76	Customer expectations	*	*	*	*	*						
77	**Local business survey**	*	*		*	*	*	*	*	*	*	
81	Factors affecting profit	*		*	*	*	*		*	*		
83	Costs and outgoings		*			*	*					
84	Increasing your own profitability				*	*	*		*			
86	Matching benefits to staff					*	*					
86	Calculating profit											
87	**Desktop**		*		*	*	*	*	*	*	*	
92	Product knowledge				*	*			*	*	*	*
93	Ways of paying	*	*	*	*	*	*	*	*	*	*	*
94	After-sales service for a car				*	*			*	*		
94	A product you wish to buy				*	*			*	*		
97	Summer holidays				*		*					
98	**Sales presentation**		*		*	*	*	*	*	*	*	
103	Being self-employed				*							
104	Partnerships – how can you tell?					*		*				
105	Limited companies					*	*					
106	Pros & cons of going public	*				*		*				
106	Famous plcs					*		*				
107	Examples of franchises					*						
107	What local authorities provide				*	*	*	*	*	*	*	
108	Right task in the right department						*		*	*	*	
111	Jobs and responsibilities	*			*	*	*		*	*	*	
111	**Chamber of Commerce competition**		*		*	*	*	*			*	
114	Role of your careers adviser				*	*						
115	Interests and suitable jobs				*	*			*	*	*	
115	Personal profile					*			*	*	*	
116	Personal questionnaire					*						
116	Suitable or unsuitable jobs?					*		*				
117	A suitable job					*		*				
118	Tasks and responsibilities	*			*	*	*					
118	Which job for Tom?					*		*	*	*	*	
120	Skills for jobs					*		*				
121	Vocational/academic qualifications	*			*	*		*				
121	Further qualifications	*			*	*		*				
122	**Newspaper article**				*	*	*	*	*	*	*	*
125	What employers look for					*						
126	All about you					*						
128	Finding out about job vacancies				*	*	*	*				
128	Ways of recruiting				*	*		*	*	*		
129	Writing a letter of application					*						
130	Filling in application forms				*	*						
131	**The careers exhibition**				*	*	*	*	*	*	*	

Index

Turn to the page number shown in **bold** in this index if you want a quick explanation of what a word or phrase means.

Academic qualifications	120-1
After-sales service	74, 93-4
Application form	32, 130
Application of Number	15-31, 86
Bar charts	18-19
Body language	11, **96**, 97
Bonuses	85-6
Break even	70
Business for charity	70
Business for profit	70, 102
Business not for profit	70
Business organisation	**68**
Careers adviser	113-5, 124
Cash	37, 43-4, 53, 55, 64, 93
Cash back	40
Cash book	34, 57, 59-62, 64
Cash flow	47, 62
Charge cards	41
Cheque guarantee cards	39
Cheques	33, 37-9, 43-4, 53-5, 93
Communication	8-14, 84
Competition	80, **91**
Computerised records	57
Conversion factors	24
Conversion tables and graphs	24-5
Co-operatives	107
Core skills	119-120
see also Application of Number, Communication, Information Technology	
Costs	**79**, 80-3
Credit cards	37, 41-4, 53, 55, 93
Credit note	46, 54
Credit side	59-62
Curriculum vitae	124, **125**, 126, 129-30
Customer expectations	74-6
Customer preference	80-1
Customer service	74-5, 84
CV	124, 125, 126, 129-30
Debit cards	37, 40, 43-4, 53, 55, 93
Debit side	59-62

Index

Decimal fractions	15
Departments	108
Diagnostic test	**116**
Direct debit	**42**
Discount allowed	62
Discount received	62
Discounts	50-1, 62
Electronic transfer of funds	42-4
Employees	**79**, 83-5, 109-10
Fixed costs	82
Fractions	15
Franchises	102, 107
GNVQ grading	6
Goods	72, **73**
Guarantees	94
Health and safety	7, 74
Incentives	85-6
Incoming payments	36, 64
Information technology	26-8
Interest	**41**
Interviews	3, 8
Invoice	17, 33, 45, 49-53, 55, 62
Job advertisements	116-118, 127
Job description	**117**, 125
Job specification	**117**, 125
Job titles	109-111
Ledger paper	**57**
Letter of application	12, 129
Liability	**105**
Local authorities	72, 107
Local businesses	71-2, 77
Logos	72
Loss	**81**
Luxuries	72, **73**
Manual records	57
Manufacturer	72
Mean	29
Measurements	21-2
Memoranda	13
Mode	29
Multinational businesses	71
Necessities	72, **73**
Outgoing payments	36, 64
Partnerships	102, 104
Paying-in slips	34, 44, 46, 54

Index

Payment received sheets	58, 63-4
Percentages	15-17, 27, 50
Personnel	**102**, 109-11
Petty cash	**37**, 45
Pictograms	18, 20
Plcs	86, 102, **106**
Presentations	3, 9-10, 89-98
Private limited companies	86, 102, 105
Private sector	102, 107
Productivity	80, 83
Profit	70, **79**, 80-1, 83-7
Profit sharing	86
Public limited companies	86, 102, 106
Public sector	102, 107
Questionnaires	5, 116
Range	30
Receipts	45, 47, 54-5
Recruitment	128
Registrar of Companies	**105**
Report writing	3, 14
Research	4-5
Retailer	72
Sales representative	**90**
Sales voucher	34, **40**
Services	72, **73**
Share ownership	**85**
Shares	85, 105-6
Sole trader	102-3
Spreadsheets	26-8, 57, 63
Statement of account	46
Study skills	2-3
Telephone skills	9
Transaction	**59**
Unique selling point	**91**
Value Added Tax (VAT)	16-17, 47, 50-1
Variable costs	82
Vocational qualifications	120-1
Wholesaler	72
Writing skills	12-14